Overrated!

Overrated!

• • •

THE 50 MOST OVERHYPED THINGS IN HISTORY

Mark Juddery

A PERIGEE BOOK

A PERIGEE BOOK
Published by the Penguin Group
Penguin Group (USA) Inc.
375 Hudson Street, New York, New York 10014, USA
Penguin Group (Canada), 90 Eglinton Avenue East, Suite 700, Toronto, Ontario
M4P 2Y3, Canada (a division of Pearson Penguin Canada Inc.) • Penguin Books
Ltd., 80 Strand, London WC2R 0RL, England • Penguin Group Ireland,
25 St. Stephen's Green, Dublin 2, Ireland (a division of Penguin Books Ltd.) •
Penguin Group (Australia), 250 Camberwell Road, Camberwell, Victoria 3124,
Australia (a division of Pearson Australia Group Pty. Ltd.) • Penguin Books India
Pvt. Ltd., 11 Community Centre, Panchsheel Park, New Delhi—110 017, India •
Penguin Group (NZ), 67 Apollo Drive, Rosedale, North Shore 0632, New Zealand
(a division of Pearson New Zealand Ltd.) • Penguin Books (South Africa)
(Pty.) Ltd., 24 Sturdee Avenue, Rosebank, Johannesburg 2196, South Africa
Penguin Books Ltd., Registered Offices: 80 Strand, London WC2R 0RL, England

While the author has made every effort to provide accurate telephone numbers and
Internet addresses at the time of publication, neither the publisher nor the author
assumes any responsibility for errors, or for changes that occur after publication.
Further, the publisher does not have any control over and does not assume any
responsibility for author or third-party websites or their content.

Copyright © 2010 by Mark Juddery
Text design by Tiffany Estreicher

First edition: July 2010

Library of Congress Cataloging-in-Publication Data

Juddery, Mark.
  Overrated : the 50 most overhyped things in history / Mark Juddery.— 1st ed.
    p.   cm.
  Includes bibliographical references.
  ISBN 978-0-399-53590-1
  1. Popular culture—Humor.   2. Popular culture—Miscellanea.   3. History—
Miscellanea.   4. Common fallacies.   I. Title.
  PN6231.P635J83   2010
  001—dc22   2010005102

PRINTED IN THE UNITED STATES OF AMERICA

10   9   8   7   6   5   4   3   2   1

Most Perigee books are available at special quantity discounts for bulk purchases for
sales promotions, premiums, fund-raising, or educational use. Special books, or book
excerpts, can also be created to fit specific needs. For details, write: Special Markets,
Penguin Group (USA) Inc., 375 Hudson Street, New York, New York 10014.

CONTENTS

INTRODUCTION

Throughout the years, many things have been rated somewhat more highly than they should have been. We once thought that leeches were a cure for practically everything. In different eras we've believed that togas, corsets, codpieces, zoot suits, safari suits, leg warmers, and conical bras were the coolest things that we could possibly wear. We have bent over backward for pet rocks, X-ray specs, sea monkeys, and Tamagotchi. We now look back and think, "Thank God we've progressed beyond that!"

But there are many things that, no matter how far we've come, remain highly overrated. These are the things that are given more credit than they deserve. We've been fed a lot of information over the centuries, and some of it has stuck. "A lie can make its way around the world before the truth has the chance to put its boots on," said former

British Prime Minister James Callaghan—and that was before the Internet.

The ancient Egyptians thought cats were divine and deserved to be worshipped like gods. Though most felines (and too many owners) would no doubt agree with that custom, we can now see that cats were perhaps a little overrated.

In the Middle Ages, alchemy was a well-regarded hobby, as the scientists of the day tried to turn lead into gold. A worthy occupation, except that it was impossible. (Fortunately, it led to modern chemistry, so it wasn't a complete waste of time.)

Some four hundred years later, gold wasn't considered nearly as valuable as tulips. Expecting the tulip market to continue rising, Dutch merchants drove up the price of tulip bulbs so high that one bulb could eventually cost more than a year's salary for the average Dutchman. In 1637, however, the market crashed, and thousands lost their life's investment. A terrible fate, but one they surely could have avoided by getting a bit of perspective. Tulips are very pretty, but why would anyone pay a year's salary for a flower? (Of course, it seems we have learned nothing from this—or perhaps after so long we simply forgot. Every so often, we have another tulip craze. Look at the dot-com boom of the 1990s, when so many people became official billionaires with online shares, then lost it all overnight: a high-tech tulip boom.)

History brings out passion—this truth rang true to me when I posted a list of the twenty-five greatest historical myths on a few choice websites. Within a few weeks, it had been read by thousands of people, and not all of them enjoyed it. The Internet, as we all know, is a place where people, hiding behind user names, feel that they can safely leave social graces behind. As a result, when you have the temerity to say that George Washington was *not* the first president of the United States (he wasn't), or that the Renaissance was overrated, you can expect a few angry replies. In some cases, people will have done their homework. (Not enough to prove you wrong, perhaps, but enough to protest vehemently.)

So I expect that a few readers will react with outrage at some of the entries in this book.

I've had many suggestions about what should be included. One friend was adamant that I include the Rolling Stones. "They're an influential and very popular rock band," I pointed out. "I don't think that history suggests that they were anything else."

"No," he said, "but they're pretty terrible."

However true that might be (or not), I've avoided making artistic judgments when compiling this list. This book is simply about things—objects, animals, events, and, of course, cockroaches—that weren't quite as useful, influential, amazing, spectacular, or necessary as we all assume. I could also talk about overrated people, but that's another topic (and perhaps a whole other book).

Call me a wimp (I've been called worse, mainly on the Internet), but I'm also avoiding religious judgments, simply because it's not my place to argue theology.

A few people also suggested that I include certain nations. The trouble is, when talking about something as wide and multifaceted as a country, it's hard to pin down how overhyped it is. Take the United States. Most Americans, however much they adore the place, admit that it isn't perfect. Texans confess that it has New York;

New Yorkers admit that it has Texas. How could something so controversial be described as overrated?

However, many of us believe that doves are friendly and peaceful creatures, seventeenth-century pirates were utterly cool, the brontosaurus was one of the most awesome animals ever to walk the earth, *Titanic* is the most popular movie of "all time" (which began, as far as I can tell, around 1966), and the fall of the Bastille was the proudest moment in French history. But many of us, I have to say, are sadly wrong—and in these pages I reveal the shocking truth.

If you're interested in discussing this, or mentioning other things that I should have included in the book, please drop a line to the "50 Most Overrated" blog at http://50-most-overrated.blogspot.com (and try to put it gently, saying things like "Dear Sir, I wish to challenge your finely argued opinion").

But of course, I don't wish to offend; I only wish to show things in a new perspective. You may never treat Oscar winners, princesses, baseball stars, or even Superman, with the same reverence.

Which is just as well. They're all just a little overrated.

Diamonds

◆ ◆ ◆

Of all the ways that you can show your undying love, few could be more ridiculous than giving diamonds. For more than a century, these transparent rocks have been deemed the ultimate gift, thanks to advertising that appeals to two things: appalling greed and extreme guilt. Why give your loved one an original work of fine art (or an excellent book like this one) when you can give her a tiny rock that fits on her finger?

And how much do these rocks cost? That's where the guilt comes in. You see, if you really loved her, it wouldn't matter. As the De Beers mining company said in a 1997 advertisement for their diamond engagement ring: "How can you make two months' salary last forever?" They may be small, impractical, and make their wearer a target for muggers, but what woman doesn't want diamonds? (That's a serious question. If you know any woman like that, please introduce me.)

For years, diamonds were the exclusive property of the rich. The nation of South Africa was built partly on diamond mines, as miners would risk their lives hoping to find these colorless rocks so that wealthy people could buy them and hide them away in safes. De Beers bought out most of their rivals to become a cartel, ensuring that diamonds were the most overpriced item since tulips. They eventually controlled 90 percent of the world's diamond supply. Instead of advertising a brand name, they could simply advertise diamonds.

But diamonds always had a problem. They may have looked good, but unlike oil or uranium, they weren't much use for anything, unless you ground them up and put them in drill bits. "Diamonds are intrinsically worthless, except for the deep psychological need they fill," De Beers's chairman Nicky Oppenheimer finally admitted in 1999.

Despite their reputation, diamonds aren't even especially rare, as vast diamond reserves have been discovered everywhere from Australia to Botswana. In the 1950s, when huge supplies of diamonds were found in northeastern Siberia, De Beers made an under-the-table deal: they would provide billions of dollars in trade to the Soviet Union in exchange for diamonds. Then they would store the Siberian stones, and the myth of diamond scarcity would remain.

The way to ensure that everyone bought diamonds, of course, was to make sure that nobody saw them as (gasp!) *common.* There was a time when, with each mother lode of diamonds discovered in South Africa, the price of diamonds would go down. In the 1870s, the industry plunged when massive diamond deposits were discovered. During the Great Depression, too many investors took their diamonds out of the safe at the same time, glutting the market. Another free fall.

In the final days of the Depression, De Beers lifted their fortunes (for decades to come) by combining two overpriced luxury items: diamonds and engagement rings. This innovation was advertised in fashion magazines. In 1948, the advertising agency N. W. Ayer & Son introduced "A Diamond is Forever," one of the world's longest-running campaigns, which made diamond engagement rings essential to anyone who even thought of proposing to someone. Of course, the idea that diamonds could last for eternity should really have lowered their market price, but like Starbucks, De Beers knew that one way to make their product more attractive was to make it exorbitantly priced. Even back in 1948, a two-carat diamond was "officially" valued at $1,000 to $3,000, which is even more expensive than a Starbucks pumpkin spice Frappuccino blended crème.

As a final touch, De Beers advertised their diamonds with some truly wretched prose: "Together, hearts light with love, they've shared their new life's happiness . . . the church so full of music and of friends, the wedding banquet marked with cake and laughter, and now, these touched-with-magic days in a world that seems their own. In the engagement diamond on her finger, a fire is kindled by such joys, to light their way through future days with hopes and memories."

Oh boy.

Of course, with such sentimentality pouring forth, nobody would be so heartless as to sell their diamonds. Hence, the company retained control of the market.

Like many great advertising campaigns, they had some

celebrity endorsements—and they didn't even have to pay for some of them. "Diamonds are a girl's best friend," sang Marilyn Monroe (whose lovers were usually rolling in money). But other songs suggest that diamonds are *not* the best thing to give your loved one, especially if you can't afford them. "Say you don't need no diamond rings, and I'll be satisfied," sang the Beatles—or to be exact, Paul McCartney (who could afford plenty of diamond rings, but obviously realized how silly they were).

Though De Beers now controls a mere 15 percent of diamond supply, the rocks are still ridiculously expensive. For this, we can thank far less life-affirming emotions than true love: greed, guilt, vanity, and shallowness. Of course, just because you love diamonds, it doesn't mean you're not a nice person. Actress Elizabeth Taylor's two main interests—apart from getting married—are sponsoring charities and collecting diamonds. She can afford to do both. If you want to declare your undying love, however, perhaps you should do it with a box of homemade chocolates, or a complete set of *Gilmore Girls* DVDs. They might not be the best gift ideas you've ever had, but they aren't nearly as dumb as diamonds.

MOST OVERRATED
FICTIONAL CHARACTER

Superman

◆ ◆ ◆

Author Harlan Ellison once said that there are just five fictional characters "known to every man, woman and child on the planet" (which is ridiculous, but let's just agree that these five guys are *really* famous). They are Robin Hood, Sherlock Holmes, Tarzan, Mickey Mouse, and . . . Superman.

In the comics, Superman is the hero everyone admires. If you're a comic book character, it is an honor just to hang out with him. In one 1985 comic, a character called him "the greatest of *all* heroes" and "the legend from whom all others have come" (all in the space of a page), echoing the thoughts of almost every other fictional character who has met him over the past few decades (and even the occasional nonfictional one, like Muhammad Ali, who once sparred with him in a "special" comic book).

Still, Superman's not so special. His true overratedness was exposed during the 2008 presidential elections. It took *Entertainment Weekly* to ask the candidates, Barack Obama and John McCain (or their publicists, at least), the *really* important question: "Who is your favorite superhero?" Obama chose Spider-Man and Batman because "they have some inner turmoil," adding that for Superman, it all comes too easy. McCain chose Batman because he pursues justice "against insurmountable odds," with no superpowers to help him.

Both candidates had a point. For all this talk about "the greatest of all heroes," it's strangely difficult to admire the heroism of someone so tough that he can survive a nuclear blast or fly through the sun without getting burned (both of which Superman has done). While Robin Hood and Tarzan fight crime with their athletic prowess, and Sherlock Holmes uses his wits, Superman has shown almost every power imaginable: super-strength, heat vision, freeze breath, and the ability to "leap tall buildings in a single bound" (and more impressively, fly). Over the years, in fact, he has exhibited whatever powers make it easy for the writers to get him out of whatever predicament they've put him in.

In the 1940s, for one comic only, Superman escaped an alien prison by merging himself with the wall. Then he contorted his face to look like one of the aliens and convinced them to go home. Meanwhile, in his popular radio serial, he could walk through walls and split into two Supermen—only when absolutely necessary, of course.

If anything, Superman's opportune powers became sillier with time. In one 1970s story, a monstrous villain demanded to fight him, just as—in his guise of mild-mannered reporter Clark Kent—he was meant to be reading the news on live television. What did he do? He grabbed one of his colleagues and used "super-hypnotism" to make the guy think that he was Clark Kent. The hapless guy then put on Clark's glasses and read the news, while Superman went out and battled the monster. Presumably, all the TV viewers were fooled as well. Comic book readers, however, must surely have known that they were witnessing one of the biggest rip-offs in comic book history (which is saying a lot).

Superman's list of powers, revealed in numerous comics over the decades, is simply tedious. When charged with electrical energy, he becomes telekinetic. He has used "super-mathematics" to correctly guess the number of beans in a jar, "super-friction" to weld metal bars together, and "super-ventriloquism" (on a few occasions) to make people think his voice was coming from another direction. He's also had unnecessary capacities like "super-landscaping" and (hoo boy) "super-weaving." Then, in the movie *Superman II* (1980), he was able to wipe his girlfriend Lois Lane's memory of his secret identity with . . . a kiss. Super-convenient. Is there any power the guy doesn't have? Well, in one story, an alien turned Superboy (Superman when he was a child) into a girl called Super Sister, thereby blessing him/her with a new power: "super-intuition." Even when not female, however, Superman has been known to rely on his "super-hunches."

Superman might be the most formidable superhero, but since his heyday, his sales have struggled against less indestructible superheroes like Batman, Spider-Man, and the X-Men. After the dark days of World War II, comic book readers were less interested in someone who could do anything, and were happy enough with someone who could thump villains. In 1993, writers tried to show Superman's vulnerable side by killing him, allowing him to be pummeled to death in a final (and very heroic) battle with an alien psychopath called Doomsday. The *Death of Superman* issue, where Superman died of his injuries in Lois's arms, made front-page newspaper headlines (in *real* newspapers, not just Superman's hometown gazette, the *Daily Planet*) and sold one hundred times the usual number of *Superman* comics.

Of course, to the surprise of few, Superman returned from the dead a few months later with some pseudo-scientific explanation. So much for a "vulnerable" hero. How can someone be called "courageous" and "heroic" when even death can't kill him? In fact, despite all his world-saving exploits, you can't help wondering why Superman doesn't do *more*. With his long list of awesome powers, the least he could do is save the environment (surely "super–global cooling" is in there somewhere), rein in the financial crisis, and stop conflict in the Middle East.

But even if he's not the greatest hero ever, there's that other claim: "the legend from whom all others have come." DC Comics, which has published Superman's adventures since 1938, often reminds their readers that, with him, they invented superheroes. Without Superman, there would be no Green Lantern, no Spider-Man, not even Captain Carrot. By 1941, he was being advertised as "The World's Greatest Comic Book Character."

Superman might be the first super-powered comic book hero, but literature was littered with superhuman good guys well before him. Nonetheless, kids in the 1930s were introduced to a new superhero. Brought up in rural, small-town America with powers far beyond those of mortal men, he was imbued from an early age with a profound sense of justice and fair play. Even as a toddler, he demonstrated great powers, so his parents taught him to keep them a secret from the world. He had great strength, bulletproof skin, and could leap tall buildings in a single bound.

Does that sound like Superman? Well, yes. But I'm actually talking about Hugo Danner, the hero of Philip Wylie's 1930 science fiction novel *Gladiator*, which predated Superman by eight years. Superman doesn't sound so blindingly original and groundbreaking *now*, does he?

Gladiator (along with the legends of Hercules) was on the reading list of Jerry Siegel and Joe Shuster, the two college boys from Ohio who created Superman. National Publications (as DC was then known) convinced them to sell the rights to Superman for a grand sum of $130—-daylight robbery, even in 1938. With Superman (along with other do-gooders like Batman, the Flash, and the Hawkman), National then started the superhero craze.

Still, other publishers' superheroes—from Plastic Man to the Human Torch to Captain America—were *not* just a bunch of Superman clones. Otherwise, National would probably have sued the pants off them. We know this because when a *real* copycat appeared (or even someone vaguely similar), National would sic their lawyers on that hero's publisher. They ended Wonder Man's career in 1939 after only one adventure, claiming that he was a Superman imitation. Fair enough, this guy had super-strength and could repel bullets and leap vast distances. He even had a big "W" on his chest.

Then there was Captain Marvel, who had similar powers to Superman, a similar cape-and-tights costume, and . . . actually, they had almost nothing else in common. While Superman played it straight, Captain Marvel had lighthearted, satirical adventures. His main crime was to outsell Superman (the first superhero to do so). With *Captain Marvel Adventures* selling more than a million copies every two weeks, National launched a lawsuit against the publisher, Fawcett. This went on for years before Fawcett gave up the ghost and stopped publishing comics in 1953.

But even though he is unreasonably powerful, even though he's spent nearly as much energy suing his rivals as he has spent defeating bad guys, we should give Superman credit for increasing morale during World War II. Even better, we should mention his 1940s radio series, in which he fought the Ku Klux Klan—defeating them on air, of course, but also exposing them to the public (complete with their code words). When "serious" radio shows were ignoring them, the Man of Steel played his part in their downfall.

On the other hand, when you have the power to move mountains (no doubt), that's the *least* you can do.

Grunge

• • •

Grunge music was a joke. No, I'm not just being a critic. One of the most popular and revered styles of rock music of the nineties—the music of Nirvana, Pearl Jam, and Soundgarden—really was . . . *a joke!* Millions of people fell for it, and are still falling for it.

"But wait a moment!" I hear you protest. "Nirvana was a deadly serious band." During the height of their success, and especially after lead singer Kurt Cobain's suicide in 1994, Nirvana—easily the most acclaimed of all grunge bands—was clearly not going to be remembered as the most lighthearted and jovial band since the Chipmunks. But Nirvana didn't invent grunge music. Grunge music was invented as . . . a joke. (Have I made that clear yet?)

Grunge was invented by Mudhoney, another band from the industrial climes of Seattle. The band's leader,

Mark Arm, coined the term "grunge" in 1982. By 1989, in songs like "Touch Me I'm Sick" and "Flat Out F—ed" (no, they were not trying to be profound), Mudhoney had perfected a simple enough recipe: mix punk with heavy metal, and add a dose of 1960s garage rock. Presto, you've invented grunge rock! As relish, name yourself after an obscure film that none of you have actually seen, and treat the music and attitude as . . . *a complete joke*. When asked whether they had a message for the kids, Arm replied, "F— the kids! Except for the ones who are buying our records! They're f—ing themselves!"

Perhaps so, but thanks to media hype, grunge became the "Music of a Generation," a response to the misery of urban life. We might assume, if we read too much *Rolling Stone* magazine or watch any of the plethora of TV documentaries about this music, that it was regarded with reverence. In fact, most of it was not critically acclaimed. But of course, there were exceptions.

Rock critics tend to agree that the best (or at least, the most important) grunge band was Nirvana, the Band of a Generation, led by the talented but tortured Cobain (the Voice of a Generation). They peaked in 1991 with *Nevermind* (the Album of a Generation), which included such songs as "Come as You Are" and the very popular "Smells Like Teen Spirit" (the Anthem of a Generation).

If grunge was the great "new" sound of 1991, rock music must have already run out of ideas. Not only was grunge music not so new—a cross between punk, heavy metal, and melodic pop—but Nirvana's "trademark" flannel shirts and faded jeans had been worn for years by the "headbangers" who listened to hard rock and heavy metal music.

Even in their performance, Nirvana just copied everything that had gone before. Rebellious cynicism? Rock stars had been doing that for years; it was part of the job. Smashing their guitars at the end of the performance? Pete Townshend was doing that in 1965. Cobain's self-destructive tendencies? Not to make light of this, but it was the oldest trick in rock music. He even committed suicide at twenty-seven (the same age that Brian Jones, Jimi Hendrix, Janis Joplin, Jim Morrison, and numerous other rock stars died). A tragedy—one that made him a "rock martyr"—but not exactly original. It has been said that every generation believes that they have invented rock music. It's strange to think, however, that the Nirvana generation, with their access to nostalgic CD collections and "classic hits" radio, could have possibly thought that there was anything remotely inventive about grunge.

So what was so special about Nirvana? Well, they had good songs. Cobain's musical hero was John Lennon. If you listen carefully, you will notice that he had a talent for writing catchy and hummable melodies ("Smells Like Teen Spirit" has been performed, in a non-grungy way, by everyone from Paul Anka to Tori Amos). Like Lennon, he had a sharp sense of humor, and like Mudhoney he tried not to take himself too seriously. Sadly, he wasn't so good at the "not taking himself too seriously" part of it.

Cobain never sought the title "Voice of a Generation," and he definitely didn't want it. "Smells Like Teen Spirit" (written when Cobain was well into his twenties) was never supposed to be as profound as most of his fans assumed. The title came after a woman told Cobain that he had the odor of Teen Spirit deodorant. "I thought she was saying I was a person who could inspire," he recalled, "and it turns out she just meant that I smelled like the deodorant."

Granted, the song still had the sort of melody you could find yourself humming on the bus. Then again, I could say the same thing about Paul Evans's awesome 1959 paean to melancholy and sexual frustration, "Seven Little Girls (Sitting in the Back Seat)."

Is that treated with the same reverence? I don't think so!

The Brontosaurus

• • •

It seems unfair to further demote the status of the brontosaurus, especially as its current status ("extinct for millions of years") is not exactly coveted. But the truth is even worse.

You probably learned that the brontosaurus, one of the most famous dinosaurs, roamed North America in the Jurassic period, some 135 million years ago. As any kid will tell you, dinosaurs are cool. They are awesome! Perhaps you had a brontosaurus in your own collection of toys, next to the tyrannosaurus rex and the triceratops.

Sadly, the brontosaurus didn't exist. It was a mistake made in 1874 by archaeologist Othniel Charles Marsh, who uncovered two sauropod dinosaur skeletons in Wyoming and thought he had discovered a new prehistoric genus. He named it brontosaurus. Marsh could find no heads among the wreckage, but as so much wisdom about dinosaurs is guesswork (the color of their skin, for example—they weren't necessarily gray), he still constructed a full-scale model, using the head of another dinosaur.

Elmer Riggs, of Chicago's Field Museum, discovered the truth in 1903: Marsh had been playing Frankenstein! The skull belonged to a camarasaurus, while the rest of the body was an apatosaurus, a creature that Marsh had already discovered. In addition it turned out that the bones he had discovered were of a young apatosaurus, whereas this so-called brontosaurus was an adult.

The camarasaurus, for the record, had been discovered by Marsh's archenemy, Edward Cope. These two paleontologists had started as friends, but professional rivalry had turned them into bitter foes, so much so that they fought over allegations that Marsh had bribed some of Cope's digging crew to smuggle key fossils to Marsh. All this one-upsmanship, however, made them unsung heroes to six-year-old boys worldwide. In their constant attempts to outdo each other, they added 136 new species of dinosaur to the nine that had previously been discovered in North America. Triceratops, stegasaurus, diplodocus . . . all were discovered by Marsh and Cope. The only drawback was that, in the rush to display their latest discoveries, they occasionally fell into the trap of accidentally inventing new beasts.

Somehow, the brontosaurus, nonexistent though it was, is today far more famous than either the apatosaurus or the camarasaurus from whose remains it was created. Scientific papers have consigned the bronto to the "mythical beasts" file for more than a century, but nobody else seems to have noticed. The brontosaurus is still one of the most famous dinosaurs, just as Sherlock Holmes and Tarzan are among the most famous humans. The common factor: they aren't real.

Doctors' Prescriptions

• • •

Doctors have one of the best reputations of all professions. They need high grades to study medicine, and their word is regarded as holy writ. For decades, nameless doctors in white coats (usually just actors, but why split hairs?) have appeared in advertisements to endorse various health products, to prove that these products are reliable and trustworthy.

Meanwhile, we are constantly warned to treat alternative forms of medicine and treatment—be it homeopathy, acupuncture, or Filipino faith-healing—with deep suspicion.

But while your GP would certainly know more than most people about which medicine to take, they do occasionally get it wrong. The medical establishment, after all, was the mob that laughed at Austrian doctor Ignaz

Semmelweis in the nineteenth century when he presented an insane new theory: that the lives of many mothers could be saved if only doctors and nurses *washed their hands* before delivering a baby. (Today's doctors see him as a great visionary hero.)

If pressed, doctors will admit that, yes, they can still get it wrong. As we all know, there are still many diseases that even a world-class physician can't cure—not only scary tropical diseases like Ebola, but also less exotic things like the common cold. Still, that hasn't stopped them from prescribing. Of course, they only have your health in mind, right? Why else would they prescribe?

Good question. Since you ask, drug companies have been terribly kind to doctors over the years. One company reportedly spent some $50,760 on a dinner at a major restaurant in Australia for three hundred cancer specialists. This was officially for "educational" purposes. But while $50,760 was especially generous, wining and dining doctors (and, frequently, offering free travel) is normal practice in the pharmaceutical industry.

Even if a doctor is highly ethical, and isn't dreaming of a night on the Caribbean as he or she signs your prescription form, the doctor still might have it wrong. There is a long tradition of this. Medical science was founded on several notions, one of which dominated medicine for nearly two thousand years. This was the theory of the four "humors" (blood, yellow bile, black bile, and phlegm), each related to one of the elements (earth, air, fire, and water) of which all matter was supposedly composed. The theory was that we stay healthy so long as the humors remain in a state of equilibrium within the body.

This brilliant discovery was from the great Roman physician Claudius Galenus, who lived around AD 200. His influence was so strong that it went practically unquestioned (just like the average GP's) for centuries, and his ideas were still used as late as the twentieth century. Why did doctors until so recently pay heed to such ancient beliefs? Perhaps it was because Galen left behind numerous texts, which stated his claims with such authority that he might as well have been wearing a white coat and appearing on TV.

In the eighteenth century, physician Sir Hans Sloane was president of the Royal Society, Britain's oldest society for the sciences. Still, he could find no cure in orthodox medicine for his niece's spinal deformity. Instead, he resorted to the healing hands of "Crazy Sal" Mapp, known as the "Epsom bonesetter." According to reports, Crazy Sal successfully treated Dr. Sloane's niece with a technique that seemed at the time like pure quackery. Actually, her work was a bit like massage therapy, orthopedic surgery, or even chiropractic treatment.

These days, of course, we know from our GPs that there is one way to treat most ailments: drugs.

This plan isn't exactly foolproof. One of the most famous prescription drug victims was Marilyn Monroe. You probably thought that her death was a suicide (or if you prefer, a CIA conspiracy), and that she took illegal substances. Actually, she didn't. Biographer Donald Spoto's research indicated that Monroe's death was an accidental overdose, caused by a mistaken prescription. If this is true, she would have been just one of many people to die in this way.

Drugs can also have side effects. In the late nineteenth century, after painkillers like morphine and codeine had proven a little too addictive, the Bayer pharmaceutical company sought a nonaddictive painkiller and cough suppressant. In 1898, they found their miracle drug: heroin (so named because it made patients feel heroic). Approved by the American Medical Association, it was soon sold over the counter at pharmacies everywhere, and sold extremely well. In fact, it was considerably more profitable than Bayer had expected. Soon, however, reports of heroin addiction flooded in. Heroin was eventually withdrawn from circulation, and Bayer didn't return to painkillers until 1913, with a new miracle drug: aspirin.

So how could the ignorant drug companies of 1898 (they didn't even know about vitamins back then!) be anything like the well-informed drug companies more than a century later? Well, advanced as they are, these companies still don't know everything. Today, if you are suffering from chronic pain in the United States, your doctor might diagnose a disease called fibromyalgia and prescribe the drug pregabalin, having decided that its benefits outweigh the side effects (including dizziness, exhaustion, and severe weight gain). Though it was only recently discovered, fibromyalgia is recognized by the American College of Rheumatology, the U.S. Food and Drug Administration, and health insurance companies. Pregabalin and similar drugs are taken by millions of people.

But if you go to another doctor, he or she might not prescribe you *anything* to treat your fibromyalgia because this doctor might believe that there is *no such thing as fibromyalgia*. "These people [patients] live under a cloud," said Dr. Nortin Hadler of the University of North Carolina, "and the more they are around the medical establishment, the sicker they seem to get." Even Dr.

Frederick Wolfe, who first defined fibromyalgia in 1990, now thinks the condition is just a physical response to stress. While the medical establishment is still at odds over fibromyalgia, we can all agree with Dr. Wolfe that drug companies are going to make a fortune out of it (and in fact, since he predicted that in 2007, that's exactly what they've done).

Meanwhile, if you suffer from high cholesterol, your doctor might prescribe you a drug called Zetia. Five million people worldwide have taken this drug, and it was worth $5 billion in 2007 alone. But early in 2008, drug companies Merck and Schering-Plough sheepishly released the (delayed) results of a two-year trial. Were there any shocking side effects? Well, yes: the drug didn't work. Zetia hadn't slowed the accumulation of fatty plaque in the arteries, which was the whole point of its existence.

With such things going on, perhaps you should just listen to age-old wisdom from your doctor: eat the healthiest food. Of course, even the definition of "healthy food" has changed over the years. Take Coca-Cola. In its early years, this blend of coca leaf and kola nut was marketed not as a carbonated, tooth-decaying beverage, but as the "Great National Temperance Drink," a healthy and legal alternative to alcohol during Prohibition in the 1920s.

Frequently, a new study seems to suggest adverse side effects of foods that are normally considered healthy, or the health benefits of foods that are usually considered "sinful." Milk chocolate, for example, probably gives you neither pimples nor cavities.

So whatever your doctor tells you, take it lightly, if only because the medical profession has a history of getting it wrong. Just remember one thing: chocolate is good for you.

◇◇

Medical Prescriptions to Ignore

GARLIC

Even food that actually is good for you might not be the miracle cure-all that doctors believe. It is said that "an apple a day keeps the doctor away" (though I'd like to know how a Granny Smith could have fought off the black plague), but it has nothing on garlic. Around 300 BC, garlic was used for dog bites, bladder infections, asthma, tumors, leprosy, and (oh yes!) the plague. It was also used, far more logically, to repel evil spirits.

LEECHES

Famously, medieval doctors would prescribe leeches for . . . everything. There was actually some logic to this. A rash of these bloodsucking creatures would lead to an iron deficiency, which could fight off the black plague. Still, the doctors overdid it slightly, making leeches the snake oil of their day. (Bloodletting is still used to treat blood diseases like hemochromatosis, so if you ever feel terrible in the morning, thinking "Ooh, I feel like I have hemochromatosis," you'll know what to do.)

TOBACCO

In 1577, soon after tobacco had arrived from North America, doctors in Europe recommended smoking as a form of medical treatment. If that wasn't bad enough, they were prescribing it to cure—are you ready for this?—*bad breath and cancer.*

GIVING UP ART

Until the nineteenth century, it was thought that tuberculosis was caused by artistic temperament. No cure there, I'm afraid.

Titanic

◆ ◆ ◆

In 1998, Hollywood producer-director James Cameron demanded that film reviewer Kenneth Turan be fired from the *Los Angeles Times* for criticizing Cameron's latest movie, *Titanic*. With *Titanic* breaking box office records and winning awards, Cameron suggested that Turan's opinion could no longer be taken seriously. Nothing to do with payback, of course.

For all of Cameron's moaning, Turan's opinions didn't make much difference. For years, we have heard that *Titanic* was the biggest film in history—by a long way. At time of this writing, it has made $1.84 billion at the international box office. It remained the "biggest film ever" until 2010, when it was finally overtaken by Cameron's next film, *Avatar* (and only three other films, *The Lord of the Rings: The Return of the King*, *Pirates of the Caribbean: Dead Man's Chest*, and *The Dark Knight*, have made more than a billion). Though *Avatar* has humbled *Titanic*'s box office record, it was also directed by James Cameron, so it obviously won't humble *him*.

Meanwhile, despite critics like Turan, *Titanic* also won eleven Oscars, matching the record set by *Ben-Hur* (1959). So clearly, it's not only the second biggest movie ever made but also one of the best. *Titanic*, therefore, is the model for Hollywood greatness.

Or Hollywood hype. Let's go over the claim of "the biggest box office earnings in movie history." Until *Titanic*, a new film was breaking the box office record every few years. But whenever the media raves about box office takings, they conveniently ignore one crucial element: *inflation*. As parents of school-age children so frequently complain, the price of movie tickets keeps getting higher. Just because a movie has made more money, it doesn't mean that more people have gone to see it.

So let's look at *Titanic*'s box office success in the fairest possible way: adjusted for inflation. Though exact foreign earnings are uncertain (and would take a math genius to figure out, which I can't afford), the good folks at box-officemojo.com have kindly calculated the most successful films at the U.S. box office. *Titanic* comes only in sixth place (with adjusted earnings of $977 million in America to date). No mean achievement, but not quite number one. Far and away the all-time most popular film is *Gone With the Wind* (1939), which, in adjusted dollars, has earned an estimated $1.53 billion in America alone. (Even outside America, where Civil War drama might not have the same buzz, it has easily outsold *Titanic*. In Britain, it broke box office records.) *Gone With the Wind* is followed by *Star Wars* (1977), *The Sound of Music* (1965), *E.T.: The Extra-Terrestrial* (1982), and one movie you almost never see on lists of the top box office earners: *The Ten Commandments* (1956).

What are the chances that *Titanic* will eventually catch up to the top three? Almost none. *Titanic*'s reign at the movie theater ended long ago, while *Gone With the Wind* fans still insist on watching it rereleased at cinemas. (One in Atlanta, Georgia, where the story was set, has been showing it since 1939.)

Of course, *Titanic* also has those much-vaunted eleven Oscars. To date, *The Return of the King* is the only other film to join *Ben-Hur* and *Titanic* in this elite club. Measured by Oscars, this makes *Titanic* one of the three greatest films in history, right?

Sort of. But even if you take the Oscars as a serious judge of excellence (and we'll talk about that later), it's worth remembering that, back in 1959, there were fewer categories. Few people knew of sound effects editing. What's more, *Titanic* had the advantage of more nominations. In three categories, *Titanic* actually lost, while *Ben-Hur* had only one loser (for the writing, which was fair enough, as you would agree if you ever listened to the dialogue).

Most of all, *Titanic*'s success on Oscar night included the award for best editing. Now I don't pretend to be an expert in the art of film editing, but I understand that Cameron was under strict instructions from his studio, 20th Century Fox, to trim the movie from its three-hour running time. Somehow, the trio of editors (including Cameron) was able to stretch it to three and a half hours, leaving several reviewers and filmgoers complaining that it was too long. What use is having eleven Oscars if at least one of them doesn't make sense?

Sports Records

• • •

Sports fans get terribly excited whenever a record is broken. It is usually described as "making history," and the athlete concerned joins "the all-time greats" (or if the commentator is really on fire, "the pantheon of the immortals"). In fact, with all of these records being broken, "a new era in human achievement" has joined the wide world of sports clichés. When a record is broken, it is big news because "the human spirit" (whatever that means) has surpassed itself.

With that in mind, let's have a sports quiz.

QUIZ QUESTION 1:

Who is the greatest 100-meter runner in history?

Based on world records, there's no contest. The greatest (male) 100-meter runner in history is Usain Bolt, who broke his own record at Berlin on August 16, 2009, running one hundred meters in 9.58 seconds. This, of course, made sports fans very excited.

But strangely, athletics devotees still might not consider him the best ever. They might insist that it's still Carl Lewis, or even (if they have especially long memories) Jesse Owens. Owens's best time (a world record in 1936) was 10.2 seconds. Lewis's best (also a world record) was 9.86 seconds in 1991. Bolt has run more than one-fifth of a second faster than Lewis ever did, and for one hundred meters, that's plenty.

So it's settled. It's Bolt, right?

Not so fast . . .

QUIZ QUESTION 2:

How often is a new sports world record set?

Quite frequently. When Donald Lippincott broke the 100-meter sprinting record in 1912, he kept it for twelve years. Nowadays anyone who breaks a record should soak in the glory while he or she can—with a few exceptions (like pole-vaulting, where the rules have been changed to make it more difficult), the record is likely to be broken again soon. The sports business, like most other businesses, is based on constant technological progress.

At the 2008 Beijing Olympics, twenty-five world records were broken in the swimming pool. Twenty-five! And that wasn't even surprising. Does that mean that the greatest swimmers in history all happened to be there? Probably not. Ask a swimming buff for a list of the all-time best swimmers. They will probably name Michael Phelps (who won about 312 gold medals at those Olympics*), and they

---

* Well, just eight actually. Close enough.

might also include recent superhumans like Ian Thorpe. But most of the people on their list—from Johnny Weissmuller to Dawn Fraser to Mark Spitz—will be people who no longer hold any records. Spitz swam a then-record time of 4:07.7 for the 400-meter freestyle in 1968, which was great at the time, but a record soon broken . . . fifteen times in the next ten years. At the 2008 Olympics, *all* the finalists were well ahead of this time (and I mean *well* ahead; the guy who came eighth strolled in at 3:44.82). In fact, the top *thirty-six* guys swam faster than Spitz. Oh, and this was one of the few races where nobody broke a world record.

So does this mean that everyone (especially Spitz himself) should stop carrying on as if he was something special? Hey, his best wasn't even as fast as Oleg Rabota (the Kazakhstani guy who came thirty-sixth with 4:02.16)!

Yet Mark Spitz's achievements were (and are) very special indeed. Sportspeople—whether running, swimming, or doing gymnastics—are simply faster, stronger, and more pliable than they used to be, so it would be bigger news if a record *wasn't* broken after a couple of years.

QUIZ QUESTION 3:
At which Olympics were starting blocks first used?

Starting blocks were introduced in 1927, but were not used in the Olympics until 1948—well after Jesse Owens had retired. Before that, sprinters dug holes in the cinders for their feet. The difference between blocks and cinders? About one-thirtieth of a second. It's like getting a good thirty-centimeter head start, which could mean a lot in a sprint race.

World records are significant, but mainly because they

show scientific advances. If they show the "triumph of human spirit" (as sports commentators keep saying), it's not just the spirit of the athletes, but also of the chemists, scientists, engineers, and researchers. It doesn't necessarily mean that we have new athletes who have swept away all who came before them.

Many nations spend millions on sports technology. Though many performance-enhancing drugs are banned (and a few records have been canceled because of this), top athletes use perfectly legal performance-enhancing supplements, not to mention high-tech outfits, equipment, medical treatment, architecture (of swimming pools and running tracks, among other things), and everything else. (In 2009, the governing body of world swimming decided that high-tech polyurethane swimsuits should be banned because they were just too damn good. For some ludicrous reason, the records broken in these suits still remained.)

Usain Bolt can run faster than Jesse Owens ever did, but what if Owens had had Bolt's training regimen, supplements, shoes, and, most of all, his starting blocks? Bolt might well be known as an also-ran.

QUIZ QUESTION 4:
Who holds the women's 800-meter freestyle swimming record?

As I write this, the women's 800-meter freestyle race record is 8:14.10, set by Britain's Rebecca Adlington in Beijing. But the record once (twice, in fact) belonged to Jenny Turrall, an Australian, who last held it (with 8:43.48) in 1975. Turrall's training regimen: swim forty-five miles a week, with no supplements or special diet, then retire while still a teenager (the usual career plan back then) because your body can no longer take the punishment.

"My shoulders were terrible, but I couldn't find a sports physio[therapist] to actually fix it. There was no such thing in those days," Turrall told me in a 2005 interview. "The kids these days have the sports psychologists, they have the masseurs, they have the doctors that are all sports-oriented . . . I used to go to this guy who'd try to do some massage on my shoulders. It was out of the garage because he was the only one that said that you didn't have to give up swimming."

And that was only thirty-five years ago.

◆　◆　◆

Of course, few knowledgeable people would argue that modern-day sportsmen like Phelps, Roger Federer, and Tiger Woods are not among the "all-time" best at their game. Yet this is not so much because they are breaking the records of the past, but because they just keep winning—beating the pants off people who use techniques as advanced as their own.

So when someone has run faster, leapt higher, or lifted more weight than anyone in history, just relax. It doesn't necessarily make them the greatest athlete of all time, and chances are, they will be surpassed within a few months. Yes, it's still a triumph of the human spirit and all that . . . but it's even more a triumph of technology.

Your Daily Horoscope

• • •

I have a confession to make: I don't know everything. Several writers believe that they know everything, and they believe that astrology is nonsense. If science can't explain it, it can't be real.

Of course, science can't pretend to have all the answers, or we wouldn't need so many scientists. Currently, there is no scientific evidence for the ancient art of astrology (which used to be considered a science), but that doesn't necessarily discredit it. For every survey that debunks astrology, another seems to give evidence that our birthdates really do influence our lives. Once I know everything, I will presumably be able to explain whether our lives are influenced (or even ruled) by the planets. In the meantime, I'll try to do what any good scientist would recommend: keep an open mind. If the moon can affect tidal patterns (not to mention people's behavior), who knows what the planets can do?*

But there's one thing that I will happily deride: popular astrology. Skeptics, of course, don't take them seriously. What's more (and here's the interesting bit), *neither do astrologers.*

These columns are based completely on the position of the sun at your birth, ignoring the planets (which, as most astrologers will tell you, are equally important). Newspaper astrology was invented in 1930, with the objective (like so much in newspapers) of simplifying a complex subject. The court astrologers, who advised kings and emperors in the hoary past, would have laughed at such a thing. Many astrologers can't stand these horoscopes because they are having a hard enough time being taken seriously as it is, without these people dividing everyone's fate into twelve groups.

Popular astrology has kept things very simple, allowing people to label everyone. "What's your sign?" is one of the first questions asked at parties—often followed by something like "Oh, you're a Cancer? I'm an Aries. Sorry, this isn't going to work." Or even "Oh boy, a Scorpio? Bad move. You'd better pretend to be something else." (I've heard that that's a problem with Scorpio. Funnily enough, I know some very pleasant Scorpios . . . but can I really trust them?)

"In a way, saying that you're a Gemini is rather like saying that you're from New York, which isn't the generaliza-

---

* Despite what skeptics like to argue, astrologers believe that it's the sun and the planets—not the stars, millions of light years away—that influence our lives.

tion it seems to be," Linda Goodman, a popular astrologer of the sixties, explained in her bestselling book *Sun Signs*. "Imagine that you're a Texan, discussing a man who is about to arrive for a business meeting. Someone says, 'He's a New Yorker,' and immediately an image is formed. He'll probably have faster, more clipped speech than a Texan, be less warm in his personal relationships, and will want to plunge into business without too many preliminary pleasantries . . . He has access to the latest plays and the best museums, so it's hard for him to remain unsophisticated."

Fine. New Yorkers are different from Texans. I'd happily agree with that, but *what does it have to do with astrology?* Do Virgos have a different accent, or eat more bagels than Libras?

Take some recent horoscopes for my sun sign (Pisces, if you must know). "If you're not getting what you want," says the horoscope in the Melbourne *Age*, "it's probably because your timing's not right." I'm sure that's correct. You really can't lose with such wisdom. Meanwhile, if you're an Aries, you can heed the advice of Alison Moroney in the *Canberra Times*: "With the sun in Gemini for the next month, your daily activities will reflect your increasing involvement with children, romance, or a special hobby." Well, that narrows it down.

(You'll note that I'm only using Australian examples here. If newspaper astrologers anywhere else provide less hazy comments, please let me know.)

Looking for a more focused horoscope, I found Adam Smith in the Sydney-based *Sunday Life* magazine. "Saturday brings clarity," he tells Aquarians, "especially when someone on your level acts as a sounding board." If clarity came to Aquarians the following Saturday, as predicted, they could have said, "Wow! My horoscope was right!" If not, then they were probably too confused to remember what their horoscope had said.

I realized that popular astrology had clearly gone too far when I saw an astrologer on television on the day of Australia's premier horse race, the Melbourne Cup, giving race tips—for each sign. She went through the zodiac, suggesting how those of each sign should bet (based mainly on their lucky colors that day).

Did anyone explain to her that . . .

No, I won't bother.

The Great Wall of China

• • •

The Great Wall of China is one of those structures so awesomely awesome that its very name fills us all with intense feelings of awesomeness. Chairman Mao Zedong said that any citizen who hasn't seen the Great Wall can't claim to be a *real* Chinese person.

Today's claim is slightly more modest: if you haven't visited the Great Wall, you haven't visited China. This actually sounds fair enough, even if it isn't true. China gets 24 million foreign visitors a year, and only 5 million visit the Great Wall. Still, in peak travel season, you could be convinced that all of those 5 million people are visiting the Wall at the same time, making it a more intimate experience than you really wanted. They are lured by the concept of a 3,900-mile-long structure, stretching across central China. The Wall that took centuries to build and protected China for centuries. The Wall that is perhaps the greatest surviving example of Oriental architecture. The Wall so huge that it can be seen from the moon . . .

Okay, calm down. I've visited the Great Wall myself, and it's pretty good once you work your way past the hordes of peddlers at the gates, desperately trying to sell you "souvenirs" like fake North Face wind jackets and papier-mâché Mongolian helmets. Still, for all its reputation, there are a few things about the Great Wall that could make us think, "What's the big deal?"

You Can't See It from the Moon

Despite the piece of trivia that people seem to mention so often, the Great Wall is *not* "the only man-made artifact that can be seen from the moon." In fact, it can't be seen from the moon at all. It *can* be seen from space, but only from a short distance. "Space" begins a mere sixty miles from the Earth's surface, where you may well catch a glimpse of the Great Wall. You can also see motorways, railways, cities, and a few buildings. From the moon, twenty-five thousand miles away from Earth, you could barely make out the continents, and any human-made artifact would be well and truly invisible. There is no point on the moon at which the Great Wall is the "only" visible man-made structure.

Somehow, this myth even made it into Chinese textbooks—perhaps to kindle a great national pride. Like the chairman, its greatness was somewhat exaggerated by the officials.

It Failed Miserably in What It Was Supposed to Do

Its *original* purpose, I mean. It's now very effective at attracting tourists, of course. But before that, it was built to be an impenetrable line of defense. That didn't work. It was breached regularly even in the early days, and the Tang Dynasty (AD 618–907) extended the Chinese empire well beyond the Great Wall, meaning that there was no longer much point to the whole structure. Still, the idea was revived a few centuries later, after China was invaded by VIPs like Genghis Khan's Mongol army. During the Ming Dynasty (1368–1644), it was rebuilt with 60 million cubic meters of bricks and stone slabs, in a project that took more than a century and incredible human sacrifice, and was guarded by an army of 1 million soldiers. So what happened next? The Manchu armies stormed the Middle Kingdom and subjected China to more than 250 years of foreign rule. You win some, you lose . . . well, when you rely on the Great Wall, you lose *most* of them.

The Great Wall eventually found its niche as an elevated highway. This was just as well, because as a fortress, it was useless.

Who Cares How Long It Is? It's Impossible to Walk the Whole Thing, Mainly as It's in a State of Appalling Disrepair

It took a long time to build the Great Wall, but even more of its long history has been spent falling apart. Ignored (understandably) during the Qing Dynasty of 1644–1911, much of it turned to dust. Built to withstand invading armies, it was somehow eroded by the weather, and peasants calmly pulled it apart to make farmhouses and stables out of the bricks and stones. If not for the tourist industry, it might have collapsed entirely. The Beijing government has even forbidden hikers from walking on the most fragile sections, which is fair enough, but also a pity because those are probably the best bits.

Most tourists go to Badaling, the section of the Great Wall northwest of Beijing, which is typically so packed with tourists that you can hardly see the pavement (unless you go in winter, when you'll freeze to death instead).

It's Not Really a Great Wall; It's a Few Reasonably Good Walls, Many of Which Are Unrelated

Archaeologists have identified walls going back to the fifth century BC. Altogether, they go 30,000 miles. That's why people think that the "Great Wall" is that long. Really, the current Great Wall stretches a relatively short 3,900 miles from east to west, including all the decrepit bits that have fallen apart (which is most of it).

But before we say, "It's such a shame that so much of the Wall has fallen" (with the mournfulness usually reserved for when great monuments and works of art are destroyed), don't forget that it was built to divide China, not to unify it. You might recall the elation in Germany at the fall of the Berlin Wall, a far more effective barrier. Look at it that way. We should *celebrate* the fact that the Great Wall of China has fallen apart miserably and no longer provides an obstacle between north and south China.

Baby Boomers

◆ ◆ ◆

The baby boomers were the generation born of returned servicemen who arrived home from World War II to start families, leading to a population explosion in the United States, England, Australia, and other allied nations. We argue over who gets to be called a "boomer," but the most common guess is that baby boomers were born between 1946 and 1964.

Nineteen sixty-four? I realize that some people started large families, but that was eighteen years after the war ended! Some of these guys must have taken nearly as long to return home as Ulysses.*

---

* According to Greek mythology, Ulysses was a hero of the Trojan War who took twenty years to return home to his wife, mainly because he was living with a foxy sorceress named Calypso and having a great time. I'm sure this is irrelevant.

The term "baby boomer" (like the younger "Generation X" and "Generation Y") is really more of a marketing term. The baby boomers grew up in the excitement and prosperity of the postwar world. They were the kids who listened to rock 'n' roll, who protested for peace and civil rights, who broke from the conservative past and into a radical, progressive future. They spoke out in their youth, changing the world as no generation of young men and women had ever done before. They were activists in the sixties and seventies, had families in the eighties, and took over the world in the nineties. (Well, a few of them did.) At time of writing, some of them are preparing for retirement.

Boomers have long been proud to be members of this generation. It has been no doubt an exciting time to be alive (and still is), but let's do the math. The very oldest boomers were not yet ten years old when rock 'n' roll hit the scene. They might have vague memories of watching Elvis Presley on television gyrating to the sound of screaming fans, but they couldn't possibly have been at the forefront of the rock 'n' roll revolution.

The oldest boomers were only eighteen when the phenomenon of Beatlemania took over the world. In 1966, when *Time* magazine bestowed its Man of the Year title on an entire generation (for the first and, so far, the only time), it was the "Twenty-Five and Under" generation. The oldest boomers were twenty, but most of the people mentioned in the cover story (from actor Julie Christie and singer Buffy Sainte-Marie to sportsman Jean-Claude Killy and decorated Vietnam hero Robert E. O'Malley) were well into their twenties.

Clearly, the boomers didn't change the world. They

simply took credit for it. The Beatles, Bob Dylan, Jimi Hendrix, and Jerry Garcia were born during World War II. Most other great cultural figures the boomers have claimed—Marilyn Monroe, Andy Warhol, Elvis, Allen Ginsberg, Jane Fonda—were born even earlier. Technically, that means they were *not* boomers.

Instead, they were part of the so-called Silent Generation born from 1925 to 1942 (or thereabouts), and named after a 1951 *Time* magazine cover story. They were too young to serve in World War II, grew up during the Great Depression and the war (in most cases), and were supposedly too anxious to be free spirits like the boomers. (Then again, by classifying them in 1951, *Time* wasn't exactly giving them much time to come of age.) Soon after *Time* started the myth, American historian William Manchester described them as "withdrawn, cautious, unimaginative, indifferent, unadventurous and silent." If Jane Fonda or John Lennon fit that description, then those words have presumably changed their meanings since Manchester's spiel.

Many of the boomers were of age in time for Woodstock and the anti-Vietnam protests, but most of them had "split the scene" (as they might have said) by the time younger crowds (mostly Generation X) were left to face the army at Tiananmen Square, knock down the Berlin Wall, and get thrown in jail for trying to save the Amazon.

But as we are still reminded, the experiences of the boomers are worth remembering. In which other generation could you listen to the Beatles and the Rolling Stones, watch *Star Trek* and *The Avengers*, dance around in a miniskirt, join antiwar demonstrations, and experiment with marijuana?

Well, actually, every generation since then—through the power of television reruns, nostalgic radio programming, retro fashion, and the fact that, despite what some people believe, the inspiration to change the world did not end with the baby boomers.

It didn't begin with them either. They just *think* it did.

The Curse of Tutankhamen

• • •

When things go wrong, we have to keep smiling. When *everything* goes wrong—morbidly, tragically wrong—we can always blame a curse. I've had days like that myself, and I'm reasonably sure that someone had put a curse on me on all of those occasions. That's the only rational explanation.

Today, the most high-profile curses usually affect people in Hollywood. What occultists and evil spirits have against moviemakers, I'm not sure, but the "Curse of Superman" has been causing trouble for almost seventy years. According to legend, the stars of Superman films and television shows are doomed to a terrible fate (which serves everyone right for making *Superman IV: The Quest for Peace*). George Reeves, who played Superman in the original TV series, took up drinking. In 1959, he either killed himself (the official story) or was murdered. Christopher Reeve, who starred in four *Superman* movies in the 1970s and 1980s, was left a quadriplegic in a 1995 horse-riding accident and died of a heart attack at the age of fifty-two. Margot Kidder, who played his girlfriend Lois Lane, was herself confined to a wheelchair (albeit temporarily) after a 1990 car accident, went bankrupt, suffered from depression, and was found living with the homeless (again, temporarily) in 1996.

Most Superman actors, however, did *not* suffer such misfortune. Kirk Alyn, the original movie Superman, lived to be eighty-eight. Teri Hatcher, who played Lois in *Lois and Clark: The New Adventures of Superman*, went on to star in the mega-super-ultra-successful *Desperate Housewives*. The evil spirit responsible must have been feeling generous that day.

Most Hollywood curses are equally far-fetched, though in moments of weakness, I'm almost willing to believe the "Curse of *Poltergeist*," which allegedly affected the cast of the 1980s movie series. When one of your leading ladies dies suddenly of a freak medical condition at age twelve, another is brutally murdered at twenty-two, and a few other actors die within two years of filming, you might consider that you're cursed (except that, in the case of the first film, you'd be Steven Spielberg, who could probably *not* be described as "unfortunate"). Being in *Poltergeist* was an even greater curse than being a regular in *Diff'rent Strokes* (whose young stars moved on to drugs, jail, and suicide). It's even worse than being in *From Justin to Kelly*. (Nobody from that movie is dead yet, as far as I know, but surely they can't be proud.) I believe in the curse, that is, until some spoilsport suggests that the deaths were merely coincidence and that *most* of the cast is still alive and well. Most "curses" don't stand up to scrutiny.

With that in mind, it stands to reason that the most overrated curse would be the most famous one: the Curse of Tutankhamen. Unlike the *Poltergeist* curse, there's no circumstantial evidence for this one. Well, not really. The famous idea of a cursed Egyptian tomb was invented by a young English novelist, Jane Loudon Webb, in her 1828 novel, *The Mummy*. Ten years after Mary Shelley invented one of the great horror monsters in her novel *Franken-stein*, Webb invented another: the walking mummy, re-turning to life to seek vengeance.

The idea of walking mummies was popular among writers of horror stories, so when explorer Howard Carter led an expedition to discover Tutankhamen's tomb in Egypt's Valley of the Kings, Sir Arthur Conan Doyle (a great believer in the supernatural and—when not pen-ning Sherlock Holmes stories—a writer of ripping horror yarns) warned of "a terrible curse." When the tomb was opened, the Cairo correspondent of London's *Daily Ex-press* wrote that Carter's team had seen an inscription that, translated from hieroglyphics, stated: "They who enter this sacred tomb shall swiftly be visited by the wings of death."

This story was complete rubbish, but it still found its way into the *New York Times* and other respected news-papers. It won extra credence a few weeks after the tomb was opened, when Carter's sponsor, the fifth earl of Car-narvon, died from a septic mosquito bite.

Believers of this curse blame it for twenty-six deaths, but despite the warning that visitors to the tomb would "swiftly" face their death, only six of the deaths occurred within the next decade. Carter himself lived for another seventeen years (which, for Tutankhamen, was almost a whole lifetime). Still, the "curse" story seems to be mentioned whenever someone happens to get food poisoning within a week of looking at an ancient Egyptian artifact at a museum. It was a hoax, people. A hoax!

Cigarettes

• • •

You might wonder what cigarettes are doing on this list. Surely, I hear you say, they can't be overrated! It's well known that they give you cancer, rot your lungs, and make your breath stink. What's more, you need to train yourself to enjoy them. While the first sip of wine or the first bite of tiramisu can be a pleasant experience, the first puff of a cigarette usually tastes awful, makes the smoker feel queasy, and is accompanied by an unpleasant cloud of smoke. Four hundred years before smoking was linked to lung cancer, King James I of England was not amused by the new weed, saying that tobacco causes "a general sluggishness, which makes us wallow in all sorts of idle delights." He called smoking "a custome Lothsome to the eye, hatefull to the Nose, harmfull to the braine, daungerous to the Lungs." He didn't need to be a regular smoker to know all that.

Nor does anyone else. We can tell from the first puff. So why do we take the second? And why, when we can all list the drawbacks of smoking (while we'd struggle to list any benefits), is it still so popular?

Make no mistake: despite all the antismoking campaigns, it's still *extremely* popular. According to the World-watch Institute, there are 1.1 billion smokers worldwide. Every year, the habit kills nearly 5 million people. "A cigarette is the only consumer product which, when used as directed, kills its consumer," said Gro Harlem Brundt-land during her term as director general of the World Health Organization.

A top secret tobacco industry memo, written back in 1961, summed up the problem: "There are biologically active materials present in cigarette tobacco. These are: (a) cancer causing; (b) cancer promoting; (c) poisonous; (d) *stimulating, pleasurable and flavorful* [emphasis mine]." Ah, now there's the twist! Also, nicotine is addictive—more addictive than valium, heroin, or alcohol. As we were told ominously at school: "Once you start, you're hooked." According to a survey by the Centers for Disease Control and Prevention, 20 percent of Americans still smoke. Houston, we have a problem.

Though tobacco was brought to Europe from South America in the sixteenth century, cigarettes were a twentieth-century trend. In 1904, cigarettes accounted for only one-twentieth of the American tobacco market. By the middle of the century, nearly half of all adults smoked. Yes, the cigarette industry is truly a great American success story.

Logically, cigarettes should have gone the way of snuff and chewing tobacco (which weren't healthy, but at least didn't have the fumes). However, the methods used to convince people to smoke cigarettes were sheer genius. Though World War I had led to a rise in cigarette smokers among men, it was the father of modern public relations, U.S. advertising genius Edward L. Bernays, who first targeted women. He promoted cigarettes as a weight-loss device, encouraging women in advertisements of the 1920s to "reach for a Lucky [cigarette] instead of a sweet," and even convinced restaurants to add cigarettes to their menus as a dessert substitute. He hired models and famous actors for testimonials. But his greatest bit of chutzpah was to make cigarettes a symbol of emancipation by organizing a group of young women to stride down New York's Fifth Avenue in the traditional Easter parade, smoking their "torches of equality." He arranged for a photographer, but it wasn't necessary; the media went haywire. The exhibition was considered shocking, not because it was unhealthy, but because women weren't supposed to smoke in public.

Thanks to PR efforts like this, cigarette smoking became very sexy. Through deals with cigarette companies, movie stars smoked copiously in their films, in some of Hollywood's earliest product placement. Humphrey Bogart was so well known for his style of smoking—letting the cigarette dangle precariously from his lips—that someone invented the verb "to bogart" (which has somehow come to mean "use up too much of the marijuana").

In 1933, the Chesterfield Tobacco Co. ran ads in a medical journal claiming that cigarettes are "just as pure as the water you drink." Ten years later, Philip Morris stated in their advertisements that smoker's cough was caused by non–Philip Morris brands (which presumably means that smoking Philip Morris is good for you). Magazine ads for menthol cigarettes focused on the dangers of smoking non-menthol cigarettes. "Unlike ordinary cigarettes," insisted one ad, "Juleps sparkle up your mouth, refresh your throat, keep your breath clean . . . even if you smoke 20–40–60 Juleps a day."

The industry hit a rock in 1950, when studies proved (or "alleged," to use the tobacco industry's PR-speak) the oft-speculated link between smoking and lung cancer. The tobacco companies combated this with their usual gusto, finding skeptical scientists—and you can find skeptical scientists for practically anything—to cast doubt on the medical consensus. Journalists were urged that there were "two sides" to the story and to cover the "controversy" with "balance." (Nowadays, the words "Iraq war" and "climate change" might spring to mind as you read that.)

Despite the creativity of the PR firms (who would invent such cool characters as Joe Camel and the Marlboro Man to persuade people to take up cigarettes), the number of smokers in the West has been falling over the past fifty years. (In 1955, more than half of all American men smoked; by 2001, it was down to a quarter.) But these days the big numbers are in developing countries, where most smokers now live.

According to the World Health Organization, half the men in these countries are smokers. In China alone, more than 300 million men smoke—and without the antismoking campaigns that have become so familiar in the West, many of them don't know the risks. One survey showed that 61 percent of Chinese smokers thought that it did them little or no harm. (For the record, one-third of all cigarettes smoked today are in China. Over there, 1.69 *trillion* cigarettes are smoked each year. You know how big a "trillion" is? Quite a lot, really.)

Just as they did in the West in the early decades of the

twentieth century, the PR people in the East are working overtime. In Sri Lanka, a tobacco company hired glamorous young women to drive around in branded jeeps and cars, handing out free product samples. In the Ukraine, the world's second-largest cigarette market after China, the state TV channel, too poor to make its own programs, showed thinly veiled ads from tobacco companies.

As for government education . . . forget it! American tobacco manufacturers, desperate for new markets as they gradually lose the domestic one, still have some lobbying power—enough for the government to threaten a number of Asian countries with trade sanctions if they didn't open their markets to American tobacco. In order to keep up, local tobacco companies have intensified their own marketing. WHO reported that tobacco advertising in Cambodia *quadrupled* in the space of four years during the 1990s.

Meanwhile, the kind of PR language that tobacco companies used in decades past has been adopted by politicians, taking a few tips from the *real* masters of hype. More than any other product, cigarettes prove that strong and clever public relations can make *anything* overrated.

Star Trek

◆ ◆ ◆

What is the greatest television show in history? Thousands, perhaps even millions, are pretty sure that it's *Star Trek*. For those who have been stranded on an alien planet for the past few decades, *Star Trek* covered the voyages of the starship *Enterprise*, which would "boldly go where no man has gone before." It showed a future where the nations on Earth had resolved their differences and were now visiting alien worlds.

You might assume that *Star Trek* was a top-rated series. In fact, when the series was first shown by NBC (between 1966 and 1969), it never ranked higher than 65 in the ratings, and only lasted more than two seasons because of an active campaign by its fans. Over the past four decades, its fans have remained devoted, even obsessive. According to one survey, a majority of Americans consider themselves

fans. If ratings are a guide, their fanaticism has rarely extended to actually watching the series.

No matter. The true fans (that is, the ones who not only
watch *Star Trek* but also buy the merchandise, attend the
conventions, and let their lives revolve around the show)
have given it a reputation as the most groundbreaking,
enlightened series in television history, placing it on a
pedestal that has convinced scores of journalists, academics, and others who should know better. Gene Roddenberry, the creator of *Star Trek*, is considered one of the
great visionaries of science fiction.

Fans even proclaim that the show's vision of the twenty-
third century gave us a brilliantly accurate view of the future. *Star Trek* "invented" mobile phones (remember those
flip-top communications devices?), microwave ovens, and
other high-tech devices. Of course, that's not exactly true.
Star Trek may have *inspired* the designs, but the science
was never explained on the show, and it was left to real
scientists and engineers to figure out how these things
could actually work. *Star Trek*'s "microwave oven" was a
device on which you could key in your preferred meal and
it would magically appear out of nowhere. I'm still waiting
for a microwave that does that.

In fairness, Roddenberry really was blessed with some
visionary ideas, and *Star Trek* would have been considerably greater if it had kept to his lofty vision. You can catch
a glimpse of this in *The Cage*, a pilot episode (written by
Roddenberry) that was not shown publicly for several
years. Jeffrey Hunter played the *Enterprise*'s impulsive
Captain Pike, whose poor judgment almost jeopardized
his mission. (Yes, a *flawed hero!*) His first mate was not
only a woman but a plain-looking, dark-haired woman

(played by Majel Barrett, later Mrs. Roddenberry). Now this was groundbreaking!

But by the time it was first broadcast, *Star Trek* had been "fixed" by NBC. Pike was replaced by the dashing Captain Kirk, whose instincts, honed through military training, could never be deemed wrong. Majel Barrett still appeared, demoted to the more traditional role of ship's nurse. Oh, and she was now blond.

Then there was Uhura, a black African woman who worked with the boys on deck, thereby inspiring several young women and girls (including comedian Whoopi Goldberg and Dr. Mae Jemison, the first female African American astronaut) to strive for higher things in life.

That was odd, because as "communications officer," Uhura made a peculiar role model for either women or African Americans. She was, in effect, a glorified receptionist whose computer panel looked strangely like a high-tech telephone call center. She also wore miniskirts (those things will always be in fashion!), looked stunning, and probably "inspired" the male viewers as much as the female ones.

In one of the series' proudest moments, Uhura and Kirk shared the first interracial kiss on American television. It is saluted as a landmark television moment—and that's exactly what it would have been, except that NBC reared its timid head yet again. On network orders, Kirk and Uhura kissed not as a sign of affection, but because aliens were controlling their minds. So it was clear: to kiss someone of a different race, you would need to be out of your mind.

The only other female regular was Kirk's lovely "Yeoman," Janice Rand, whose role seemed somewhere between secretary and concubine. So in a series renowned for its female role models, we had a nurse, a receptionist, and a personal assistant. All very worthy and noble jobs for any gender, but surely females will branch out of their stereotyped roles in the next two hundred years.

Then there were the story lines: in almost every episode, Kirk (an American) teleports down to an alien planet with his first officer, the alien half-breed Mr. Spock (whose mother was American) and Dr. "Bones" McCoy (another American).* They take one or two other guys (usually also Americans) to be killed by whatever is down there.

Much has been said about the multicultural crew, but the non-Americans (Chinese, African, Scottish, and later, Russian) usually had little to do but obey their captain's orders. Their foreign policy, as they beamed down to each planet, left something to be desired. "Captain Kirk was always talking about the 'prime directive,' which was the order the crew of the *Enterprise* had received never to interfere in the affairs of other planets," wrote David Brooks in Britain's *Weekly Standard* newspaper. "But they interfered in almost every episode and almost always in the same way: they disposed of tyrants and created democracy."

Ah, so that's how you make a Utopian future! The problem with *Star Trek* lay not in Roddenberry's famous pacifism (like many of his writers, he was anti-Vietnam), but in the bullheaded way that his characters attempted to improve the universe.

Then again, what would I know? I'm a *Doctor Who* fan.

---

* It was never clear why the ship's doctor would beam down with the captain and first officer. Perhaps the advanced medical technology of the time left him with nothing else to do.

"Yankee Doodle"

• • •

The most overrated song would surely have to be something patriotic. The Libyan national anthem still cheerfully advises its people to "seize the forehead of the tyrant and destroy him," while the Luxembourg national anthem has contagious lines like "Where slow you see the Alzette flow, the Sura plays wild pranks." When people sing such lyrics with patriotic zeal, you know that patriotic songs are truly ridiculous.

Before we go on, I should admit that I live in a country where the song that really inspires us to nationalistic fervor is "Waltzing Matilda," a ballad about a sheep rustler who kills himself when the police track him down. It was on the short list in 1977, when citizens were actually allowed to vote for the national anthem. They chose the nineteenth-century ballad "Advance Australia Fair." Of course, back in 1977, Aussies were also taken by the sounds of Leo Sayer and the Bee Gees. Nowadays, it's difficult to find many Australians who will admit to liking their anthem (which proudly announces that "Our home is girt by sea," whatever that means, but I'm not sure why we should be so proud of it). Indeed, most Aussies don't know the song beyond the first verse. "Waltzing Matilda," however, is something that we can sing all the way through.

The United States, of course, has many far more sensible patriotic songs, from Irving Berlin's "God Bless America" to Woody Guthrie's "This Land Is Your Land" (written as an alternative to Berlin's song, for less religious types). Oh, there's also the national anthem, Francis Scott Key's "The Star-Spangled Banner," which took its melody from a crass English drinking song, "To Anacreon in Heaven." Its origins were so unsavory that Congress refused to endorse it as the anthem for more than a century, until its unofficial status was exposed in a 1929 edition of the newspaper cartoon *Ripley's Believe It or Not*. This led millions of people to sign petitions that were sent to Congress, and "The Star-Spangled Banner" was made legit in 1931.

Happily, Key's lyrics are far less dubious than the melody. That leaves "Yankee Doodle," the great pre-Revolutionary marching song, to snatch the title of America's most overrated song. With its catchy melody and (usually) light drumbeat, it has motivated American troops since soon after it was written in 1758, which is very impressive, because it doesn't really make any sense.

For those two or three people who don't know, the song is about a pony rider who sticks a feather in his hat and calls it "macaroni." And you thought the Aussie sheep rustler was dumb! What sort of twit would mistake a feather for a type of pasta? In fact, Italian food wasn't so well known in America back then, so very few of Yankee Doodle's countrymen could possibly have known what he was raving about.

Fortunately, this book is here to get to the bottom of even the most baffling parts of American history. Hence, I can reveal that the lyric was probably a reference to the Macaroni Club, an eighteenth-century club of bewigged, decadent young men who aimed to bring European exoticism to Europe—and as the name suggests, this included Italian pasta.

It wasn't meant to be flattering. "Yankee Doodle" was meant to slander the American Revolutionary troops. So how did they react? They took it as a source of patriotic pride! Huh? Hey, we Aussies might sing proudly about a suicidal criminal, but at least "Waltzing Matilda" was written by a famously patriotic Australian (the great A. B. "Banjo" Paterson, the closest we've ever had to a poet laureate), rather than the enemy. Don't you guys know when someone's dissing you?

Experts say that "Yankee Doodle" was written by (or at least adapted by) a British Army surgeon, Dr. Richard Shuckburgh, just before the joint British/colonial attack on Fort Niagara in 1755. The colonials didn't have the neat, orderly uniforms and the high-class weaponry of the English, so Shuckburgh used the song to criticize the colonials' lack of style, antiquated hardware, and lack of military training. Yes, even when they were fighting on the same side, the British were abusing the colonials. And they thought the *Americans* had no style!

At the time, the colonials had the good sense to be

infuriated, and changed the lyrics to their own end, with the catchy title "The Farmer and His Son's Return from a Visit to the Camp."

The word "yankee," a nickname for Americans in general, would of course be used as an insult by the Confederate States during the Civil War. The Confederates might have had a point, as the word was possibly a Native American corruption of *anglais* (the French word for "English"). How insulting can you get?

Still, the British continued to tease the colonials with their own versions of this dopey song, rather obnoxiously playing it in front of Boston churches during services. The lyrics were rather cutting for the time, especially (one imagines) for anyone in prayer:

> *Yankee Doodle came to town,*
> *For to buy a firelock.*
> *We will tar and feather him,*
> *And so we will John Hancock.*

By that stage, the very tune was enough to make fun of Americans. On the way to the battle of Concord, the redcoats reportedly marched to this song, hoping to demoralize the colonials. As both sides kept responding with their own versions, Britain's General Thomas Gage heard it so often that he said, "I hope I never hear that song again." Many have doubtless shared his sentiments over the years.

If a Briton tries singing the song to you, with the sneering tone in which it was intended, I'm afraid I can't think of any American-penned ditty that will insult him back with the same power. Fortunately, their own national anthem does a good enough job. If you go as far as the sixth verse, the perennial "God Save the Queen" shows its age with the lines:

> *And like a torrent rush*
> *Rebellious Scots to crush.*

And with that, they offend 10 percent of their own population. Way to go!

December 25

•   •   •

It's surprising how many people still believe that December 25—Christmas Day, for those who have somehow avoided this knowledge—is actually the date that Jesus was born. Some believe that the reference to the Star of Bethlehem, which guided the shepherds and wise men to the baby Jesus, has been used by astronomers to figure out the date. There is in fact nothing, biblical or otherwise, to suggest that he was born on that day.

So why do we celebrate Christmas on December 25? Of the many different theories, perhaps the most likely is that the day was already celebrated by followers of Mithras, the central god of a Hellenistic cult that developed in the eastern Mediterranean around 100 BC. Almost no texts from the era exist, but ancient reliefs and friezes seem to indicate that followers of Mithraism believed that Mithras was born on December 25, probably the son of a virgin, and his birth was attended by shepherds.

There are other similarities. Mithras also had twelve disciples; Sunday was his sacred day; he was buried in a tomb and rose again after three days. When scholars investigated Mithraism (relatively recently, in the early twentieth century), they upset some Christians by suggesting that Mithraism may have influenced Christianity. (Then again, Mithraism continued—developing and perhaps changing its beliefs—for some centuries after Christ. Some of the influences may well have been in the other direction.)

So when was Jesus really born? Let's return to the Star of Bethlehem. Based on this star, astronomers have figured out that he was born on September 11, 3 BC. (Yes, *September 11.*) Historian Dr. Ernest L. Martin, in his 1981 book *The Birth of Christ Recalculated*, even went so far as to suggest that the signs in the sky on the night of Jesus's birth could only have happened on September 11 between 6:15 p.m. and 7:49 p.m. Unfortunately, he couldn't be any more exact.

If the late Dr. Martin was correct (and Jesus didn't happen to be born, through some astounding coincidence, on Mithras's official birthday of December 25), then it's not the only thing that most of the world gets wrong about Christmas. There's also the belief your relatives seem to have that you desperately need socks and neckties.

More important, there is the idea that Jesus was born in a manger. Yes, the Gospel according to Luke makes three references to a manger, but as any scholar (or at least, a few linguistic scholars) could tell you, the Greek word translated as "manger" in these passages is derived from the verb meaning "to eat." Ergo, the word means "feeding place." This could have been a trough, but it could far more likely have been the court of an inn or a tavern. As it was probably not December 25 (and hence no Christmas crowds), chances are there was enough room at the inn. (In AD 165, St. Justin wrote that Mary and Joseph could find no lodgings in town, which is why they sought—and found—shelter at a tavern in the neighboring town of Bethlehem.)

So, apart from the Holy Family, there is little in the Bible to conjure images of the traditional nativity scene. No cows, no sheep. The Bible suggests that, apart from the Holy Family, only the angel was present. Nativity scenes often have a few other details wrong too. Despite describing them as ascending into heaven, none of the biblical scribes ever suggested that angels have wings.

Yes, the shepherds showed up a little later, as did the wise men.

But were there three wise men? Surprisingly enough, the Bible never mentions how many there were. Three gifts, yes, but we don't know how many wise men were there to present the gold, frankincense, and myrrh to the baby Jesus. And despite Christmas carols like "We Three Kings," none of the Gospel writers ever said that the wise men were kings. The works of early Christian writers, in fact, suggest that they were Persian astrologers, which explains why they'd follow a star.

So there you have it. In a few short paragraphs, I have just crushed your long-standing beliefs about Christmas. Sorry about that. (If it's any consolation, Santa Claus actually did exist, though he might not have used flying reindeer or said "Ho ho ho!") But if this is a little sad for those who have long enjoyed nativity plays and paintings of the newborn Jesus being watched lovingly by cows and sheep, spare a thought for those born on Christmas Day: only one set of presents each year, upstaged by Santa Claus and the roast turkey . . . and they can't even claim to share their birthday with Jesus (if that matters to them).

Still, Christmas births have often been presented as something special. Publicity for the Hollywood star Humphrey Bogart always listed his birth date as Christmas Day 1899. Clifford McCarty wrote in *The Complete Films of Humphrey Bogart* that Warner Bros. Pictures had changed Bogart's birthday from the less romantic date of January 23, 1900, to "foster the view that a man born on Christmas Day couldn't really be as villainous as he appeared to be on screen." (Before he became a leading man in *The Maltese Falcon* and *Casablanca*, Bogie usually played bad guys.)

This would have been one of Hollywood's strangest publicity decisions. Stars were meant to fit their on-screen personae, so "softening" one of their tough guys with a Christmas birthday seems to defeat the purpose. Why did they do it?

Answer: they didn't. In reality, Bogart's Christmas birth date was not a Hollywood myth. The myth (spread by writers like McCarty) was the "fact" that it was Hollywood myth. Got that? Many Hollywood stories, strangely enough, are actually true. Bogart really was born on Christmas Day.

The list of Christmas babies is impressive: geniuses (Sir Isaac Newton), nation builders (Mohammad Ali Jinnah), cosmetics tycoons (Helena Rubenstein), entertainment legends (Cab Calloway, Rod Serling, Little Richard, Sissy Spacek, Annie Lennox) . . . So if you take pride in the celebrities who share your birthday (and statistically, most people do take pride in such things), there are still plenty to choose from on that date.

Hemlock

• • •

Socrates, the great philosopher, had a good death. According to his foremost disciple, Plato, he was sentenced to death by poison, very calmly drinking a cup of hemlock. When his friends and disciples bawled their eyes out, Socrates said, "Really, my friends, what a way to behave! Why, that was my main reason for sending away the women, to prevent this sort of disturbance; because I am told that one should make one's end in a tranquil frame of mind. Calm yourselves and try to be brave."

Just before he took the hemlock, Socrates was instructed: "Just drink it, and then walk about until you feel a weight in your legs, and then lie down. Then it will act of its own accord." He followed these instructions, and died peacefully—according to Plato.

Hemlock, for the record, is a drink made from a poisonous plant in the parsley family. (The plant itself can be used medicinally, as a *very* powerful sedative.) Based on the story of its most famous victim, hemlock seems like a good way to go.

Or perhaps not. Plato presumably wanted to assure Socrates' followers that their master's death was a peaceful one. But despite chronicling this death, he wasn't one of the fourteen disciples who were there to witness it. He claimed that he was ill, but some historians have unkindly suggested that he deliberately stayed away, hoping to distance himself from the controversial and generally unpopular Socrates. It might be fitting that Plato's account of the trial was called the *Apology* (which is from the Greek for "defense," but is still fitting in modern English). His account of the last day of Socrates' life (including his death), *Phaedo*, was narrated by Phaedo, a possibly fictitious young disciple of Socrates. Plato never suggests that he himself was present, and Phaedo is in fact depicted telling his story many years after the event. British translator and scholar Hugh Tredennick's belief that the final scene is "impregnably authentic" (I guess he wasn't interested in a debate) might not be exactly right.

Sadly, Socrates' death was probably not so painless. Most other people who have been poisoned by hemlock have suffered from convulsions, nausea, vomiting, paralysis, and a generally nasty, agonizing end. The only part that fits with Phaedo's version is the paralysis. Of course, Socrates was an inherently spiritual man—it's been suggested that he was enlightening the West in the same way Gautama Buddha was enlightening the East a century earlier—so he might have faced death with meditative peace. But if he could achieve such serenity with hemlock coursing through his veins, he had probably (like Buddha) achieved the fabled state of nirvana.

Unfortunately, very little can be proven about Socrates, the father of philosophy. Socrates himself never wrote anything (and even if he had, we can assume he wouldn't have reported his own death), and Plato's accounts of his life were inconsistent and unreliable. We don't even know what distinguished Socrates' philosophy from Plato's contribution. We know all about hemlock, though. And it's very nasty.

Fortunately, not many suicidal people have read Plato's account, and there have been very few recent cases of death by hemlock. Take my advice: don't kill yourself by drinking that noxious brew. (In fact, I should advise that you don't kill yourself with *anything*. But I'm sure that goes without saying.)

Bra Burning

• • •

Whatever you may have heard about the women's movement, it didn't suddenly appear out of nowhere in the sixties, but gradually developed over a number of centuries. It wasn't until 1968, however, that feminists allegedly performed one of their most famous rituals: burning their bras. Most of the ringleaders in the women's movement of the time were not crazy (despite some media portrayals), but intelligent, dedicated, focused individuals. As such, they probably didn't do anything as silly as bra burning.

The first "bra burners" were a group of about a hundred women who showed up outside the 1968 Miss America pageant in New Jersey shouting "Freedom for women!" while holding placards saying "Women's Liberation" and "Let's Judge Ourselves as People." After getting the media's attention by crowning a live sheep "Miss America," they threw various beauty products—girdles, false eyelashes, hair curlers, tweezers . . . and bras—into their "Freedom Trash Can." They allegedly wanted to set them on fire, but since they were standing on a wooden boardwalk, the police advised them not to do so. Fortunately, they listened.

The myth of bra burning has been traced to that day, particularly to an article for the *New York Post* by a young journalist, Lindsay Van Gelder. "I mentioned high in the story that the protesters were planning to burn bras, girdles, and other items for the Freedom Trash Can," she recalled to *Ms.* magazine in 1992. "The headline writer took it a step further and called them 'bra-burners.'"

When flicking through newspapers, many people simply read the headlines (and if the headlines are interesting, maybe they'll move on to the first paragraph). Therefore, media across America took the imagery and ran with it. Even the *Washington Post* talked of women who "burned undergarments during a demonstration."

I have not found any evidence of anyone burning a bra for the cause of freedom. (Then again, how does a guy research something like that without being thrown out of the library?) The myth was so famous, of course, that someone was bound to do it eventually (hopefully *after* removing her bra). If someone did, chances are that she would have suffered for her principles. Women of my acquaintance (or at least, the ones I was game enough to ask) assure me that they wear bras for their own personal comfort. True, the bra also prevents their breasts from sagging (which is presumably why it was labeled a "beauty product"), but that, I understand, is a secondary reason. All that bra burning would have achieved would have been the chance for women to show off some of their undergarments for a few seconds, which doesn't really seem like a very feminist thing to do.

Robin Morgan, leader of the Miss America demonstration in 1968, later had regrets. She believed, in retrospect, that they seemed to be attacking the contestants rather than the contest. The contestants were meant to be shown as the victims, but when you stand around singing "Ain't she sweet / Making profit off her meat" (as the protesters did), that point might not be so clear.

It certainly brought attention, but it possibly wasn't the greatest demonstration in the history of feminism. For all its flaws, however, it could have been worse. They could have burned their bras.

The Great Fire of London

• • •

The Great Fire of London in 1666 destroyed 80 percent of the city, left one hundred thousand people homeless, and caused an estimated $17 million of damage—a lot of money in those days. That all sounds very nasty, so what, pray tell, is it doing in this book? The fact is that, as far as "great" disasters go (especially those that are still talked about more than 340 years later), it was very wimpy.

It's true! The fire spread remarkably slowly, killed only a handful of people, and seems almost harmless compared to many lesser-known fires. London was swiftly rebuilt (even by modern building standards), and almost all the people who had lost their homes were rehoused within a few years. Most namby-pamby of all, the fire probably *saved* thousands more people than it killed. You call that a disaster?!

The Great Fire of London was started early in the morning of September 1, 1666, by an oven in the bakery of Thomas Farynor, royal baker to King Charles II. So where were the emergency services? When alerted to the fire on the first night, the lord mayor, Thomas Bludworth, took one look and retired back to his room, muttering that it was so puny that "a woman could piss it out." Diarist Samuel Pepys wrote that he protected his valuables by burying his wine and cheese in his backyard. (Yes, you read that right.)

Proving that London had too many flammable objects (and too much dry wind), the fire burned for five days, destroyed thirteen thousand homes and eighty-seven churches, but allowed many of the people living in the area to calmly evacuate to a nearby shantytown. Unlike the fierce summer fires of the American forest or the Australian bush, which can travel a few miles in a matter of minutes, this one gave everyone plenty of time.

Of course, people were still killed directly by the fire. But how many? A thousand? Three hundred? Seventy-six, perhaps?

Just five recorded deaths, actually. Farynor's maid was unfortunate enough to be too close to the oven, as was a nearby watchmaker. One man died of smoke inhalation outside St. Paul's Cathedral. Two others, trying to rescue their prized possessions, fell into their cellars. That's five! Even the Woodstock music festival killed more people than that. (More on that later.)

Later, the fire claimed another victim when a crazy (and presumably suicidal) French watchmaker, Robert

Hubert, claimed responsibility. There was no evidence that Hubert had done it (quite the opposite, in fact), but Londoners needed a scapegoat, and were intent on blaming Catholic extremists from France. He was hanged, and his corpse was torn to shreds by an angry mob.

London's previous major fire, back in 1212, left three thousand people dead, and you've probably never even heard of it. London wasn't such a world-class, "happening" city back in the medieval world. Just as we often struggle to remember natural disasters that claim tens of thousands of victims in developing nations, while mourning incidents that take three or four of our countrymen, history has implied that the 1666 fire counts for more because by then London was a cultural, political, and economic center.

To be fair, the "Great" Fire of London destroyed two-thirds of London and left millions in a state of abject terror. Though only five deaths were recorded, there were indirect deaths like the nutty Hubert and a few killed in the street violence (as people lost their senses). Later, hundreds died from exposure, as they had been made homeless and were forced to sleep in open fields. So I can't exactly go around saying that the fire was a *good* thing, can I?

Oh, yes I can! Despite its reputation as one of the darkest, most terrifying moments in British history, it actually did more good than harm.

The fire shook Charles II out of his state of decadence, forcing him to be a caring, diligent king. Unlike the plague, the fire showed no more compassion to wealthy citizens than it did to the poor. Historian Gustav Milne later suggested that Charles had reason to fear that "the

Great Fire could rekindle the Great Rebellion." Charles stepped in to help, becoming a volunteer firefighter and, once the wind had blown the fire to the Thames, helping to rebuild London. In the end, the Great Fire of London must surely be seen as a textbook case in how *not* to destroy a city.

Carrots

• • •

Now, don't get excited, kids! I'm not one to say anything against such a fine vegetable as the carrot. But it's time we set the record straight: their natural, fresh goodness has frequently been overstated. During the Middle Ages, for example, they were used as a treatment for everything, including snakebites and sexually transmitted diseases. Sadly, they didn't work.

A few hundred years later, they were overrated even more highly by World War II propaganda. For decades since, children have been told that carrots are good for their eyes.

The idea was popularized by Britain's Royal Air Force, which circulated the rumor that some of their crack pilots, shooting down enemy planes, owed their outstanding night vision to carrots. In truth, it was a new invention called radar, but they wanted to keep this technology a secret, lest it fall into enemy hands.

With all this talk of the wonders of carrots, the English started growing and eating more of them so they could see their way through their houses during the blackouts that had become essential to save them from enemy raids. The government did its best to encourage the public's love for "these bright treasures dug from the good British earth," distributing recipes for such delicacies as carrot marmalade and sweet carrot flan.

Of course, carrots don't *harm* your eyes. They contain beta-carotene, a chemical compound that is rich in vitamin A. This vitamin doesn't improve your general vision, but prevents night blindness, meaning that your eyes take less time to adapt to changes in the light. Still, this doesn't make them the optical wonder food we have all heard about.

However many carrots they ate, the people of England didn't suddenly pull off their glasses yelling "I can see! It's a miracle!" In fact, while they would have been getting more than sufficient doses of beta-carotene, they would have had even more if they'd been eating apricots, blueberries, kale, or spinach.

Don't get me wrong, we should still eat our carrots. But as they don't really deserve most of their reputation, you don't need to have so many, and you can start focusing on other vegetables, like broccoli and Brussels sprouts. Sorry about that.

Woodstock

◆ ◆ ◆

"It was unique in that there were a half-million people not stabbing each other to death at a concert, and that hadn't been done before."

—Grace Slick, lead singer of Jefferson Airplane, demonstrates her knowledge of musical history

There are some places, usually starting with "W," that are bywords for a mood and an event. "Watergate" is a Washington, DC, hotel complex, but since 1973 it has been forever linked with government corruption and all-American shame. "Waterloo" has come to mean the defeat of a seemingly unbeatable opponent. "Woodstock," of course, means peace, light, and hedonism. Chances are, if not for famous historical events, we would never have heard of these places.

The strange thing is, these famous historical events didn't even happen at these places. Sure, the Watergate affair included a breaking and entering in the hotel complex, but more of it happened behind closed doors at a certain other address: 1600 Pennsylvania Avenue. Napoleon was not defeated at Waterloo, but four miles away, at a point between the villages of Plancenoit and Mont-Saint-Jean. The Woodstock Music and Art Fair, whatever the name suggests, was not held in the town of Woodstock, New York, but in the rural town of Bethel, an hour's drive from Woodstock.

But that's not the only thing people get wrong about it.

Woodstock is near the top of many people's "I wish I was there" lists—four days of peace, love, and togetherness, as five hundred thousand people flocked to a six-hundred-acre dairy farm to witness a free, one-of-a-kind concert by the greatest rock artists of the time (except the Beatles . . . and Bob Dylan . . . and the Beach Boys . . . and the Rolling Stones . . . and—look, it still had a lot of big stars, okay?). It was an optimistic, idyllic call for the future.

Or so you may have read. Actually, the whole thing was arranged not as a harmonic gathering, but as a profit venture. (Some performers, including Janis Joplin and The Who, refused to perform on Saturday night if they weren't paid in advance.) Conceived by a couple of yuppies in suits (yes, they had yuppies back then, they just didn't have a name yet), the tickets were pricey, which is why so many people opted to save money by breaking in. To make it easier for gate-crashers, it was so badly organized that ticket booths never made it to the entrance. "All we ever got to move was two or three," said garage-owner Ken Van Loan, who'd been hired to tow the ticket booths into position, in a later interview with the *New York Times*. "Each one we moved took longer and longer. There were too many people and cars and abandoned tents blocking the way." By the time the security team came in, it was already out of control. Naturally, Woodstock lost millions, meaning that, as far as its organizers were concerned, it was a terrible failure.

The journey to heaven, as we all know, can be arduous. Ditto the journey to Woodstock, with a traffic jam so long that many of the first-day acts were stranded, leaving the first performer, folk singer Richie Havens, to perform for nearly three hours (including seven encores, whether or not he or anyone else wanted them). He finished by improvising an anti-Vietnam War song, before his replacements were finally flown in by U.S. Army helicopter. "It was the only helicopter available," recalled Havens in 1984. "If it wasn't for the U.S. Army, Woodstock might not have happened . . . We were never anti-soldier. We were just against the war."

Even the music wasn't so good. The Grateful Dead, plagued by technical problems, described it as their worst-ever performance. Others, such as Joan Baez and Ravi Shankar, had to deal with rainstorms. Jimi Hendrix's performance has become the stuff of legend, but he didn't perform until the final day (after the program was officially over), and by that time most people had left.

The true magic of Woodstock, however, was that you could completely ignore the music and *still* have a terrible time. "Like Kennedy's Camelot, Woodstock has been retrospectively lifted to epic lore," wrote columnist James Campion in 1999. But for those who found themselves there, it was nothing short of a disaster area. The Who's Pete Townshend still speaks of it in chilling terms. Filmmaker Martin Scorsese (who was assistant director on the Oscar-winning documentary *Woodstock*) has often compared it to surviving war. The difference was that there was little or no violence in Woodstock, but that might have been partly because, due to the poor security, most people were too stoned.

According to rock historians (and man, there are a lot of them!), the peace and hope of Woodstock was ruined four months later when the Rolling Stones were inspired to organize a free festival (unofficially called "Woodstock West") at the Altamont Speedway in California. Unlike Woodstock, this concert was actually held in the spirit of altruism. Sadly, it is part of rock folklore that the security guards (members of the Hell's Angels gang) were too tough and killed one of the revelers when he became troublesome. Two other concertgoers died accidentally. It was the end of the fantasy.

But despite Altamont's notoriety, Woodstock actually had more casualties. Of Woodstock's 5,162 medical cases (including 797 documented instances of drug abuse), two died of heroin overdoses. Another concertgoer was crushed in his sleep by a cleanup tractor. The attendant medical director, Dr. William Abruzzi, said that there were also eight miscarriages in the Woodstock medical tent. Okay, nobody was beaten to death, but eleven deaths and miscarriages isn't quite as good as, say, *none*.

"We had passing coverage of the music," said Al Romm, editor of the *Times Herald-Record*, recalling his newspaper's reporting of Woodstock. "Really could have done better with that. We were just enveloped with the human indignities, the sickness, the miscarriages."

Whether or not you enjoyed it, Woodstock probably would have been an interesting experience (provided you brought your own fresh drinking water and had some accommodation nearby). But perhaps it wasn't as meaningful and important as people think. Still, to many of the sixties generation, it was their Great Event, their answer to the Armistice or the fall of the Berlin Wall. But those events really *did* change the world order. Woodstock didn't really do so. Most of the hippies at Woodstock stopped being hippies before 1979.

Which might not be a bad thing. Peace and love are wonderful things, but can they be achieved through leaving your hair unwashed, breaking into concerts, listening to rock 'n' roll, and engaging in large amounts of drugs and sex?

If so, we would probably have them by now.

The Oscar

◆ ◆ ◆

It might seem strange to put the Oscars in this book. After all, they have more than their share of detractors. Every year, movie buffs and critics moan about them getting it "wrong" because their own favorite films or actors didn't win, or complaining that they are too predictable (even if they just lost money betting on the wrong winners).

But despite all the criticism, the Academy Awards (or Oscars) are the most coveted of awards, even among people who haven't made any movies. When the media covers a prestigious award in any field, be it aviation or furniture design, it is often described as "the Oscars" of that field. As some people have noted, an Oscar winner can guarantee how his or her obituary will begin. There are some exceptions (Al Gore and Bruce Springsteen, for example), but generally, the death notices of everyone from Steven Spielberg to Tatum O'Neal to the woman who did the makeup for *Elizabeth* will be prefaced with the words "Oscar winner."

But the Oscars, quite simply, can't be taken seriously.

For starters, many people consider them the world's most prestigious film festival. This isn't really true, simply because they were conceived to specifically salute Hollywood films. The masterworks of Fellini, Kurosawa, and Ingmar Bergman were never in the running for "best picture." It's relatively recently that foreign films have been nominated for the major awards, though no foreign-language film has yet been named "best picture" by the voters (unless you'd count *The Godfather, Part II* and *Slumdog Millionaire*, which were basically English films with substantial foreign-language segments).

Does an Oscar really mean that someone is the best filmmaker? Not necessarily. At least, no more than winning an election would make someone the best leader. Like political parties, the big studios spare little expense in campaigns to win Oscars (and even nominations), spending up to $1,500 per voter. And every year, movie critics treat the whole thing with cynicism. The road to Oscar glory, they often note, seems to be based more on politics than excellence.

When critics want to show how ludicrous the Academy Awards really are, the film that they most frequently pick on is *The Greatest Show on Earth* (1952), directed by Cecil B. DeMille, about a group of touring circus performers. It had an all-star cast, including James Stewart in clown makeup and Betty Hutton as an emotional trapeze artist. It is not quite as awful as critics suggest, but it isn't anything exceptional either. But it somehow managed to win the Oscar for best picture of 1952. A bad year for movies? Actually, it was the year of *Singin' in the Rain* (which won *nothing*, and wasn't even nominated for best picture), *High Noon*, and *The Quiet Man*, films that are now considered by critics and others to be "all-time classics" (whatever that means).

So who is responsible for such bizarre choices? The Oscar winners are decided by members of the Academy of Motion Picture Arts and Sciences. This is a diverse bunch: mostly white, American, male, over sixty. (The Academy has often been accused of being too "safe," winning controversy by trying to avoid it.) However, while they might enjoy the same chardonnay, they probably don't meet in a top secret hideout to decide the results, whatever critics might imply when talking about how the Academy decides the Oscars.

In fact, most members of the Academy are as clueless as anyone else. I interviewed one in 2001—the late actor Ron Randell, then eighty years old and unable to remember most of his career. The Oscars had been awarded a week beforehand, and I noticed that he had video copies next to his television of many of the nominated films, sent to him by the studios.

He revealed that he had never seen any of these films, didn't know anything about them (and didn't even know how to operate his video player), but voted anyway. For whom? He couldn't remember. Did he vote for his fellow Australian actor, Russell Crowe (who had won that year for *Gladiator*)? He frowned: "Russell Crowe . . . The name rings a bell. I *might* have voted for him."

There are many other stories, at least some of which are

probably true (like the one above). Henry Fonda's widow once said that he always let the maid fill out his Oscar ballot. Dancer-actor Ann Miller said that she seriously considered not voting one year because of the "sloppy appearance of the actresses" who were nominated.

Of course, the voters might well be influenced by the campaigns. Harvey Weinstein, as founder of Miramax Films, was often blamed for turning the Oscars into a political election, since his studio began its aggressive lobbying for films like *The Crying Game*, *The Piano*, and *Pulp Fiction*, promoting these films for voters as art house masterpieces. (None of them were named best picture, but they all did rather well at the Oscars.) Miramax finally won a best picture award for *Shakespeare in Love*, which also won a best actress trophy for Gwyneth Paltrow. To show how much of a political contest this had become, Miramax had engaged in the kind of negative campaigning that would make the U.S. elections seem nice, attacking Paltrow's competitors (including Emily Watson, Fernanda Montenegro, and especially Cate Blanchett) for the terrible crime of not being American.

While Weinstein might have had them down to a fine art, Oscar political campaigns have been going since at least 1930 (the second year that the awards were presented), when the powerful actor-producer Mary Pickford invited the voting committee to an exclusive party at her mansion. Result: she was named best actress for *Coquette*.

But for all these stories, the Oscars are still seen on television each year by hundreds of millions around the world. Of course, many of those people are more interested in the gowns than in the awards themselves. (In many countries, the red-carpet entrances get better ratings than the awards themselves, perhaps because it's a quick and easy way to see the stars in designer glamour while avoiding the long, drawn-out awards ceremony.)

But how important is it? Well, an Oscar can boost your career greatly, but it won't necessarily save you from obscurity. Remember F. Murray Abraham, named best actor of 1984? (*Amadeus* was the movie.) Remember that the first actress to win two Oscars (in subsequent years, no less) was not Katharine Hepburn or Bette Davis, but a woman named Luise Rainer? No, I didn't think you'd remember.

Hopefully, the voters are swayed by quality, not hype. Then again, these are the people who decided that *The Greatest Show on Earth* was "better" than *Singin' in the Rain*. Fortunately, in the history of cinema, we remember more than just Oscar winners.

Why *Not* to Win an Oscar

MARY PICKFORD

Pickford, Hollywood's most popular silent film star, lobbied to win an Oscar for her first talking picture, *Coquette.* Not her smartest move. *Coquette* was one of her worst-reviewed movies and would have been better ignored. It's difficult for anyone to ignore your movie, of course, if it wins you an Oscar. Her career would never recover.

LUISE RAINER

To the surprise of everyone, including herself, young Luise Rainer was the first actress to win two Oscars (within two years). While it may have been a great honor, it didn't do her much good. Within a year, after some less successful films (which typecast her as a dewy-eyed innocent), her career fizzled. "I have often heard the Academy Award to be a bad omen," she later said. "I don't think it need be. Except, maybe, that the industry seemed to feel that having an Academy Award winner on their hands was sufficient to overcome bad story material as was, often, handed out afterwards to stars under long-term contract." Still, her Oscar may have had fringe benefits. A study noted that Oscar winners live longer than nonwinners, and the more Oscars the better, it seems. At the time of writing, one-hundred-year-old Rainer is the oldest living Oscar winner.

MARISA TOMEI

When the cute young Brooklyn-born actress won the 1993 best supporting actress award for her scene-stealing role in *My Cousin Vinny*, many film buffs were flabbergasted. How could she have beaten distinguished nominees like Joan Plowright, Vanessa Redgrave, Judy Davis, and Miranda Richardson? It was unkindly suggested that, upon opening the envelope, seventy-four-year-old presenter Jack Palance didn't actually read it, but spaced out instead, repeating the name of the last nominee. For the record, the winners of each award are also known to two officials, who are stationed in the wings, so one of them would have ostensibly stepped up to the podium and announced the winner before the flub became an official result. (Then again, as this has been the practice since 1953, I'm amazed that we've never seen it happen.) But how could Tomei have won against such a prestigious group? Well, the Academy is famously patriotic. The British vote would have been split, but as the only American nominee, perhaps it would have been more surprising if Tomei had *not* won. Nonetheless, Tomei's name is still mentioned ruthlessly when buffs want to talk about the "least deserving" Oscar winners (despite having two critically acclaimed nominations for later films). Her career also faded after her Oscar, boosting rumors of a "curse" of Oscar-winning actresses. (This is Hollywood. Of *course* there was a curse!)

◇◇

Princesses

• • •

Blame Mother Goose, whoever she was. (It's still not certain.) While we're at it, blame the Brothers Grimm, Hans Christian Andersen, Walt Disney, and anyone else who inspired us to grow up with fairy tales. Thanks to them, we seem to have a peculiar adoration for princesses. Something about these privileged women makes us look upon them as pristine, enhanced beings. They are regarded as even more special than movie stars, without having to do nearly as much work. Many women want to be princesses, swept away by their own Prince Charming (or at the very least, a billionaire Arabian prince with his own fleet of jumbo jets). What could be a more worthy dream?

Princesses might be glamorous (with all their wealth, they can afford to be), but there are a few things we should remember about them:

Princesses, like most royalty, are usually irrelevant.

In fact, even in centuries past when royalty carried far more clout, princesses were generally irrelevant.

Princesses don't actually do much.

Sleeping Beauty, you might recall, spent most of the story—her *own* story—in a deep sleep. This is one thing that the fairy tales got right. Most princesses, by virtue of their status, haven't led very active lives. Princess Maria Theresa (consort of Louis XIV) spent most of the day stuffing herself with chocolate and garlic sauce. With such nauseating habits, it's no surprise that she died at forty-five.

Let's face it, most princesses are boring.

True, sometimes they have interesting habits—from the wild life of Princess Stephanie of Monaco to the disgusting personal hygiene of Princess Maria Giuseppina (consort of the proudly homosexual Louis XVIII of France, who lived on another floor of the palace to avoid her)—but when that happens, they are less than perfect, which defeats the whole purpose of being a princess.

Princesses are not always as beautiful as in the fairy tales.

Genetics isn't class-conscious. Princesses were often married to princes for political reasons, not because the prince wanted a lovely wife. Bavarian princess Marie Anne Victoire was notorious for her ugliness. Happily, her prince, the eccentric French Louis the Grand Dauphin, was turned on by ugly women (seriously!), so they lived happily ever after.

Princesses haven't always been as nice and sweet as their reputation suggests.

Take Cinderella, perhaps the most popular princess in history (despite being fictional). In most versions—from Charles Perrault's 1697 story "Cendrillon" (on which most later versions were based) to the 1998 movie *Ever After*, starring Drew Barrymore with a perfect English accent (which was very impressive, except that Cinderella was French)—Cinderella has been the ultimate tale of a heroic struggle against the odds, a stepdaughter abused by her ugly stepmother who meets her handsome prince. But in earlier versions, before she was softened, Cinderella was a calculating, sinister go-getter who killed her first step-mother so that her father would marry the housekeeper. Her famous plight, in which she was forced into slavery by her overbearing stepmother and pampered stepsisters, was probably just what she deserved.

Sleeping Beauty, meanwhile, was perhaps not as blessed as you think. True, in the earliest known version of the story, she marries a prince (and as with most versions, manages to do it with minimal effort). But he didn't wake her with a kiss. Instead, this fine, upstanding charmer raped her as she slept, then went back home to his wife. Sleeping Beauty was woken from her sleep by the kicking of her twins in her womb. In the prince's first act of re-sponsible behavior, he took mother and children to the palace, where his wife tried to kill them. The king stopped this, and Sleeping Beauty ended up married to her rap-ist. Within the rather dubious morals of the age, this was known as a happy ending.

As for the heroine of *The Princess and the Pea* . . . well, that story hasn't really changed since Hans Christian Andersen wrote it. She is still perhaps the most pampered, precious wimp in the history of fairy tales (despite all that competition from her fellow princesses).

◆　◆　◆

Royalty is not nearly as overrated as it used to be, but princesses still have an appeal as magical (and as ridiculous) as anything in a Disney movie. Take the most popular member of the British Royal Family of the past twenty years: the late Princess Diana, the "People's Princess."

Diana, of course, really *was* a special case (and not just because she divorced her handsome prince). She dedicated much of her life to charity and saw her role model as Mother Teresa rather than Cinderella. Princesses who use their position for such activities should certainly be commended. But as Diana would quickly and graciously point out, many less famous, less privileged people dedicate most of their lives to charity, in between earning a living. They just do it in cheaper clothes.

Seventeenth-Century Pirates (Especially of the Caribbean)

• • •

As any kid will tell you, nothing could be cooler than being a pirate on the Seven Seas . . . apart from being a superhero, perhaps. (Sadly, I haven't found any evidence that costumed superheroes really exist. I'm still searching, though.) Sailing the high seas, robbing and terrorizing victims, living a life of chaos and danger—what could be more fun? It was like the eighteenth-century equivalent of being a rock musician!

Unfortunately, for most of their careers, Blackbeard, Captain Kidd, and their cohorts were not nearly as rebellious and rule-breaking as their notoriety would suggest. In fact, they worked as privateers, commissioned by nations to attack other nations' ships. Yes, governments actually put them on the payroll, and it worked well for those governments. The commissioning country didn't have to pay for a navy. In fact, England hired privateers for years, before they had a large naval fleet of their own. The privateers could even show the Letter of Marque, issued by the government to show that they were *legally* pillaging and plundering. This meant . . . what? Nobody was allowed to fight back?

Whatever the case, it made piracy considerably less rebellious and exciting than its reputation would suggest. Privateering was like getting a government grant to play loud, obnoxious rock music or spray graffiti all over the walls (which has happened with a few art grants, of course).

Seventeenth-century pirates usually didn't acquire their treasure by attacking wealthy ships, but by trading coffee, tea, slaves, textiles, and stolen medicines on the black market. (But to reinstate at least some of your romantic images, I should emphasize: it was on the *black* market.)

This was one way for criminals to go straight without actually behaving themselves. English privateer Henry Morgan was hired as commander of a privateer fleet, due to his previous experience as a noxious, fearsome pirate. With the "nudge nudge, wink wink" knowledge of the British government, he led a multinational raid against a Spanish stronghold in Puerto Principe, Cuba, in 1668. Now for some real piracy, right?

Not really. The raid yielded little booty, and nearly half of Morgan's men deserted him.

During the so-called Golden Age of Piracy, between 1680 and 1730, privateering was still a proper job. But it was now a little more exciting. The Golden Age began after a papal ruling that granted Spain and Portugal exclusive trading rights in the New World. A nice arrangement for them, you would imagine, but Spain just wasn't satisfied. Instead, it demanded that non-Spanish vessels seek a license to operate in North American waters. Thus started a privateering war, which was probably the only thing that ever made a pirate's life resemble one of those old Hollywood adventure movies.

Otherwise, the scurvy dogs of the Caribbean were remarkably civilized. True, they robbed their victims, but they didn't terrorize them. When a ship was captured, a captain was usually executed only if he was known for tyranny or for mistreating his crew. "To pirates, revenge was justice; punishment was meted out to barbarous captains, as befitted the captain's crimes," wrote historian Marcus Rediker in *Villains of All Nations*. Non-barbarous prisoners from other vessels were usually free to leave after a short while, or join the crew if they so wished (which had its benefits).

During the Golden Age, pirates even had a pirate government. Yes, far from the dog-eat-dog world of folklore, they were highly democratic, making efforts to prevent dictatorial control. Whatever you might have assumed, pirate captains won their positions through election rather than through violence, which actually made them far more democratic than most governments back in those days. Naturally, their crews didn't join a union (that would just be silly), but then, they didn't need to. The booty was divided evenly by the ship's quartermaster, and if the crew had a grievance, they would take it to pirate court to settle in a civil fashion.

By now, you're probably wondering: how could *anyone* be so civilized, let alone a pack of mangy brutes on the high seas? Actually, it gets worse, or to be more accurate, *better*. Embarrassing, really.

You see, not all of the booty was shared among the crew. No, a little was left aside as welfare for needy pirates and as insurance for pirates injured in accidents or battles. In fact, they lived better than your average sailor, with more food and more time to sleep. Unlike the crew of His Majesty's *Bounty*, pirates were generally not known for mutiny. Indeed, while the *Bounty*'s Captain Bligh was allowed considerable power, major decisions on a pirate ship were put to a majority vote, as stated by pirate law.

So if you find yourself in the eighteenth century, and you want to live an unruly and chaotic life on the sea, mutineering and killing innocent people, then I suggest you join the Royal Navy. Don't be a pirate; they were boring.

◇◇◇

The Truth About Those Pirates

CAPTAIN KIDD

A wealthy family man, law-abiding citizen, and former pirate catcher, he was so bad at this job that he became a privateer, raiding ships for the British government. Even this career change didn't work out, and he was brought to trial because the ships he attacked were not French. For political reasons, he was portrayed as a fearsome scourge of the seas by opponents of the Whigs (the party that sponsored his expedition) and was executed. His reputation remains, in all its inaccuracy.

BLACKBEARD

Blackbeard (Edward Teach), the most mangy, fearsome pirate ever to sail the seas et cetera et cetera, started his career as, yes, a privateer. After the privateering war ended, he beat unemployment by doing what he did best, and fortunately it was now highly illegal, which aided his "cool" credentials immensely. When he was finally captured, the British Royal Navy confiscated his treasure. Diamonds? Sapphires? Whiskey, perhaps? Not exactly. Try 145 bags of cocoa, twenty-five hogsheads of sugar, a bale of cotton, and a barrel of indigo. Oh, Blackbeard, you wild man, you!

BURIED TREASURE

Blackbeard is also famous for one of the great pirating legends: buried treasure. When the navy asked him where he kept his real treasure, he allegedly replied, "Only the devil and I know." For the past 260 years, treasure hunters have scoured the coast of North Carolina (his pillaging hub) with metal detectors, hoping to find jewelry, gold doubloons, or at the very least, pieces of eight (Spanish silver coins). So far, no luck. Conclusion: Blackbeard probably invented the treasure to impress people.

WALKING THE PLANK

The coolest form of pirate punishment, it is also a highly impractical and time-consuming way to dispose of prisoners. Fortunately, there is no real evidence that pirates did this. If they wanted to dispose of their enemies, they would often just throw them overboard, as any sensible killer would do. Walking the plank was first mentioned in a storybook in 1837, more than a century after the Golden Age ended.

CAPTAIN JACK SPARROW
A fictional character. Ditto Bluebeard and Long John Silver. Get over it.

◇◇

Sgt. Pepper's Lonely Hearts Club Band

◆ ◆ ◆

When music critics or aficionados list the "all-time" greatest rock albums, they will almost invariably mention the Beatles' *Sgt. Pepper's Lonely Hearts Club Band* (1967). Remember when you first heard *Sgt. Pepper*, and how much it changed your life? Well, no, I can't (but then, I wasn't around back in 1967).

Normally, when a work of art is described as one of the "all-time greatest," its reputation has been built over time. *Hamlet*, Beethoven's Fifth Symphony, *Citizen Kane* . . . none of them were thought of as "the greatest" when they were unveiled to the public. *Sgt. Pepper*, however, was immediately hailed as a masterpiece. The Beatles made the cover of *Time* magazine, and many paragraphs were spent analyzing the impossible-to-ignore cover (which, for those two or three of you who haven't seen it, shows the Beatles in their colorful marching-band uniforms, surrounded by wax dummies and cardboard cutouts of many famous people). The songs were also vastly different from the pop songs with which the Beatles had made their name.

So you can understand the excitement. The greatest, most popular band in the history of rock music was experimenting with new styles of music. *Sgt. Pepper* was nothing like anything that they had ever recorded. The gimmicky cover and the unusual songs meant that even tone-deaf people could notice that the album was something special.

Somehow, the hype has continued for the past four decades. *Sgt. Pepper* has gone down in history as the album that started art rock and the hippie movement (which is not necessarily a reason to be proud). Serious rock fans, however, know that it was just one of a number of albums from the era—from the Beach Boys' revered *Pet Sounds* to *Forever Changes*, by the Los Angeles band Love—that deserve credit (or blame) for such things.

Let's go through the ways people keep describing *Sgt. Pepper*:

"The album that changed music."

The Beatles were on the cutting edge. What that means is that they were listening to a lot of other influential musicians. They cited *Pet Sounds* as a major inspiration for *Sgt. Pepper*. Early in 1967, they witnessed a talented new guitarist, Jimi Hendrix, from a private box in the Saville Theatre in London, and were occasionally seen at London's psychedelic UFO Club, watching up-and-coming bands like Pink Floyd (who in fact recorded their first album at the Abbey Road Studios, just as the Beatles were doing *Sgt. Pepper*). Due to the Beatles' popularity, *Sgt. Pepper* was easily the most famous and bestselling of the "new" rock albums, but the most influential? It was a follower as much as a leader.

"Truly profound and meaningful lyrics."

Whether or not it's the greatest rock album, it's certainly one of the most pretentious, and perhaps this wasn't the fault of anyone who was actually involved in the recording. We can safely assume that more words have been written about *Sgt. Pepper* than any other rock album. "Whole lives have been wasted trying to divine messages in Beatles songs, playing records backwards and the like," wrote journalist James Button. According to "experts," "A Day in the Life" compares a bad acid trip with a good one. References in "For the Benefit of Mr. Kite" to "Mr. Kite" and "Henry the horse" were code for heroin, of course. As for "Lucy in the Sky with Diamonds" . . . everyone knows it means "LSD."

The Beatles themselves never confessed to such cleverness. In fact, they denied a lot of it. "A Day in the Life" merged two incomplete songs: one by John Lennon, one by Paul McCartney. Lennon took the words to "Mr. Kite" (including the "daring" reference to Henry the horse) from a Victorian circus poster he found while browsing through an antiques shop. Even "Lucy in the Sky with Diamonds" was innocently named after a drawing by Lennon's son Julian, featuring one of his classmates. John devised a bizarre, dreamlike world (often compared to Lewis Carroll's *Alice's Adventures in Wonderland*) to match Julian's artwork. It was Julian who gave it the title—which makes sense, because the initials of the title actually spell

"LITSWD." As an adult, Lucy herself was tracked down by the media and won some short-lived fame for her role in history. (Everyone who played some obscure role in a Beatles song is deemed worthy of media coverage.)

Of course, it was probably still drug-inspired. The Beatles, as we know, took drugs like they were going out of fashion, and this helped to make them very fashionable indeed. So certain phrases in *Sgt. Pepper* ("I get high with a little help from my friends") probably were about drugs. The weirdness in "A Day in the Life" was about . . . drugs. "Fixing a Hole" was perhaps about . . . drugs.

So this was the deep, hidden meaning of *Sgt. Pepper*: drugs. This is fine, but not exactly profound. Wasn't this album meant to be *profound*?

In between recording sessions for *Sgt. Pepper*, the Beatles recorded songs like "I Am the Walrus," which was nonsense. Literally. Bored with all these people listening to his songs and analyzing their "hidden meaning," Lennon strung together several meaningless lyrics so that pretentious schoolmasters and university professors could rack their brains working out what it all meant. (Happily, it had the desired effect.) Nonetheless, some Beatles fans, well aware of Lennon's fiendish plan, still insist that it does mean something, even if Lennon himself didn't know. Come on, guys, get over it!

From *Sgt. Pepper* on, people started looking for some hidden meaning in Beatles lyrics and album covers. This peaked with the famous "Paul is dead" rumors, in which overimaginative fans noticed numerous subtle hints of Paul's death. These started, of course, with *Sgt. Pepper*. The back cover photo of the band showed McCartney with his back to the camera. Proof that he was dead? No, he just wasn't available for that shoot.

Fans saw more clues in other songs and album covers, until eventually a few people were shocked to find Paul alive and well. They still haven't found enough evidence, however, to disprove many of the other theories that have made *Sgt. Pepper* the most overanalyzed rock album in history.

"The greatest music ever!"
That's what many people believe—and of course, we are all entitled to our own opinions. But just out of interest, have any of them heard anything by Bach?

Doves

• • •

You might have learned the biblical story in school. After it had rained for forty days and forty nights, Noah sent forth a dove, "to see if the waters were abated from off the face of the ground." Unable to find land, the dove returned. Seven days later, Noah released her again, and she returned in the evening with an olive leaf in her mouth, proving that the waters had abated (and that olive trees can grow in almost any environment). Seven days later, he sent forth the dove once again, "which returned not again unto him any more."

From this story, doves somehow became a symbol of peace: the dove with the olive branch told Noah that God was ending his "war" with humanity. (Apart from the few He'd saved, most humans were dead, so He'd already won. This shows that God is smarter than you think.) Turtledoves, especially, have been used in numerous poems and songs as objects of love (maybe because "dove" rhymes with "love," which also explains why so few love songs mention ostriches).

Alas, doves are far more vicious than their reputation suggests. Austrian animal psychologist Konrad Lorenz placed a male turtledove and a female ringdove in a cage together, then left for a few days. The sight that greeted him, upon his return, was not for the squeamish. The turtledove was prostrate on the floor, a bloody mass, having lost a fight with his mate. She was now pecking away at his remains. Not a good thing to give your true love on the second day of Christmas, or any other time. When Buddy Holly sang that "you give me all your loving and your turtle-doving," we might not have realized exactly how exciting his relationship was.

This was an eye-opener for Lorenz. Even wolves will stop short of killing each other in a fight. Lorenz concluded that predatory animals, equipped to kill their food, will not kill each other. Animals that are equipped to fly away, however, have no such built-in conscience.

When we're not waxing lyrical, we can see doves for what they truly are: pigeons. Suddenly, they don't seem so romantic. As any New Yorker (such as Woody Allen) could tell you, they are "rats with wings," known for their poor hygiene and notorious capacity for defacing statues.

Doves may not be the most vicious creatures on Earth, but they are far from the legendary harbingers of peace we know them to be. In fact, they might well be the most overrated animals since the days when the ancient Egyptians worshipped their cats.

The Fall of the Bastille

◆ ◆ ◆

Nations seem to have a problem choosing their national holidays. Australians celebrate January 26, the day white settlers landed in New South Wales and started to take over. (It is known as "Invasion Day" by some of its many critics.) America, of course, celebrates the Fourth of July, even though only one of the Founding Fathers signed the Declaration of Independence on that day, and *official* U.S. independence wouldn't happen for another seven years.

But the world's most overrated national holiday would have to be France's Bastille Day: July 14.

As every Frenchman knows, the Bastille prison in Paris was a symbol of injustice and oppression in pre-Revolutionary France, where enemies of the king were held in terrible conditions for their political beliefs. When the people stormed the Bastille on July 14, 1789, they freed hundreds of prisoners from the yoke of a cruel and tyrannical monarchy. And so on.

The organizers of the French Revolution had several talents. Among them, they could create propaganda with as much skill as any oppressive regime. Thanks to them, Louis XVI's consort, Marie Antoinette, lives on in popular mythology as a callous, pampered bimbo who, when the peasants complained that they had no bread, dismissed them with the line "Let them eat cake." (She almost certainly didn't really say that, and if she did, she would have been quoting an earlier passage from Jean-Jacques Rousseau's *Confessions*.) Thanks to the revolutionaries, a song originally written for the king's army, "La Marseillaise," became the rallying call for the revolutionary cause (and eventually the national anthem), even as the songwriter was languishing in prison.

With such propagandists on their side, it was a simple matter for the fall of the Bastille to seem like the start of French independence (which it probably wasn't) rather than a chaotic and unnecessary mistake (which it most certainly was). Yes, Bastille Day, France's national day, commemorates . . . a mistake. Oh, those wacky French!

The Bastille was an obsolete medieval fortress located in a working-class section of Paris. It had been a jail for centuries and had indeed housed the occasional political prisoner. Voltaire, imprisoned after offending the authorities, wrote his first play, *Oedipe*, there in 1718.

However, when it was raided in 1789, the Bastille held just seven prisoners, and none of them, as far as we can tell, were there for political reasons. Still, it was a handy focal point for a demonstration by the sans-culottes, mostly impoverished members of the working class, who resented the National Assembly, and demanded increased wages, fixed prices, and "more bread."

The mob, which included some defecting soldiers, marched on the Bastille to arm themselves with the prison's supply of muskets. The governor, Bernard-René de Launay, refused to hand over the weapons, leading to a lengthy stalemate. The rioters eventually forced open the outside gates. Though he could have taken them with his armory (and destroyed most of the district), de Launay took the peaceful option and surrendered on the promise of safe conduct.

Instead, the demonstrators stormed the prison, releasing the seven detainees and dismembering the Bastille's guards. A hundred people, both soldiers and civilians, died in the attack, including de Launay, whose head was carried through Paris on a pike, and several guards, mostly exsoldiers, "invalided" from regular military service. Okay, the demonstrators were angry, but they weren't exactly behaving any more humanely than the rulers. Who were the bad guys here?

For the record, the newly free ex-prisoners were the Comte de Solanges (imprisoned for "sexual misdemeanor"), four forgers, and two lunatics, including a Major Whyte, who hailed from either England or Ireland and thought he was Julius Caesar. Were they overjoyed to be free of the shackles of tyranny? Probably not, and not just because they were insane. The Bastille was fairly cozy, as prisons go, with relaxed visiting hours and decent furniture. Prisoners were given a generous spending allowance, plenty of tobacco, and were even allowed to keep pets. "The wine was not excellent, but it was passable," wrote former inmate

Jean Francois Marmontel. "No dessert: it was necessary to be deprived of something. On the whole I found that one dined very well in prison."

Had the peasants known this, chances are that they would have stormed the Bastille simply to break into this fine establishment, which was considerably more pleasant than the world outside. Instead, they destroyed the fortress stone by stone. What a waste.

To suggest that they had actually achieved something by destroying the Bastille, hideous engravings of prisoners languishing in chains next to skeletons were soon for sale on the streets of Paris. The story of the fall of the Bastille spread, portraying the mob as noble innocents driven to desperation by the tyranny of the Bastille, while the soldiers—many of whom had died in the line of duty—were wicked instruments of this injustice and oppression. The story also suggested that the seven freed prisoners were political prisoners. Whatever the case, it was a sign that the revolution had begun. A pity that, of all the great moments of the Revolution, the French choose to celebrate one of the dopiest.

Baseball

• • •

Now it's time to name the most overrated sport. In Australia, where I'm writing this, it's probably cricket. In a few nations, this terribly British sport is a national obsession. We care passionately about who wins the cricket World Series, even though, in most of the world, nobody could care less. A "proper" cricket game is quiet, slow-moving, and lasts for days. I believe that the winner is the spectator who stays awake the longest. "I watched a cricket match for three hours waiting for it to start," quipped Groucho Marx.

In America, nobody has been willing to stay awake through a game of cricket. Instead, the title of Most Overrated Sport belongs to a sport that is related to cricket: baseball. Like cricket, it isn't nearly as important as its fans—or their nations—seem to think.

In 1977, a group of U.S. sports editors and writers were polled on the greatest male athletes of the century. The top 15 was comprised entirely of Americans, and five of those were baseball players (including the top 2). Baseball was easily the most represented sport on the list. Perhaps this says less about the greatness of the game than the narrow-mindedness of sports writers back in 1977 (or any other time).

But then, this is a game where the World Series is played only by American and (in more recent years) Canadian teams. Even the World Cup events of hockey, rugby, and rock-paper-scissors (yes, that's a real event) invite competitors from more than two nations. Hey, even the World Series of *cricket* has more nations than that! But in baseball, many fans tend to forget the rest of the world. For the past century, the sport has boasted a few "all-American heroes," from Jackie Robinson and Joe DiMaggio to perhaps America's best-loved sportsman, Babe Ruth. It is one of the few sports whose "national" heroes are a bunch of guys who only played against their compatriots.

This means that Ty Cobb (1886–1961), as one of America's most gifted players, also gets to be called a "national hero." Cobb was more than just a ballplayer. He was also an unhinged, violent sociopath who beat up his wife, fellow players, newsmen, and on one occasion, a crippled fan. He pushed a chambermaid down the stairs (possibly because she was black and he was, allegedly, an appalling racist). Only through baseball (or on special occasions, warfare) could such a creep ever win national hero status.

How tough are baseball players anyway? Back in 1982, various researchers figured out the physical demands of various sports, putting them on a scale from one (for more relaxing, if no less skillful, sports like billiards, golf, and water-skiing) to ten (Tour de France cycling) and beyond (the super-tough pursuit of decathlon went off the scale). On that scale, baseball made it to a relatively wimpy *three*: slightly tougher than cricket, on a par with roller derby and scuba diving (if that's actually a sport), but not as tough as most other sports. Whatever their salary, the average baseballer isn't as tough as the average ice-skater, fencer, surfer, or jockey.

What's more, despite being America's national sport, baseball isn't even American. It was probably invented in England, where it is first mentioned (as "base ball") in 1744. This is a sensitive issue—so sensitive that, in 1907, former National League president A. G. Mills devised a myth that it was invented in 1839 by Abner Doubleday, who would go on to be a Civil War general. (The real General Doubleday, one of Mills's classmates at West Point, had gone on to a magazine writing career. Baseball was not among his topics.)

Happily for those who take it seriously, baseball has widened its horizons since the days of Babe Ruth. It even became an Olympic sport in 1992, when Cuba (whose dictator, Fidel Castro, was a former elite baseball player) won the gold medal. The United States didn't field its strongest players, who were too busy making millions in the (ahem) World Series. Still, like surprisingly many Olympic sports, baseball is far from "international" and is only a major sport in Japan and (some of) the Americas. In fact, it was removed from the Olympics program after 2008. Curling and synchronized swimming can stay; baseball can't.

So enough of the all-American obsession, not to mention the way baseball is so often used as a metaphor for life. "If I have to enjoy another self-important spew on the lofty significance of this national pastime that is past its prime, I'm going to hurl," wrote *Sports Illustrated* journalist Michael Silver in 2001. "The people who try to sell baseball as life need to get one."

Cockroaches

• • •

Cockroaches are tough little blighters. They have been around for 280 million years, and it's difficult to get rid of them. Even if you pull their heads off, they can still survive for a couple of weeks. If they're really starving, they have no qualms about eating each other. As you have probably heard, they can even survive the Big One—a nuclear bomb attack. Yes, they certainly are tough.

For those who can't stand the little pests (and that's most of us), good news is at hand. Despite the myth, cockroaches probably won't inherit the Earth in the event of nuclear war. They will outlive humans, but that isn't saying much. When exposed to radiation, humans would die after only 400–1,000 degrees of radiation (rads).

Insects are far more resistant. Back in 1959, Dennis A. and Martha L. Wharton exposed several insect species to radiation, and found that 48,000–68,000 rads can kill wood-boring insects, 64,000 is enough for a fruit fly, and 180,000 rads would kill a parasitoid wasp (of the genus *Habrobracon*, for those biologists and show-offs among you). But a mere 1,000 rads could render a cockroach sterile, and as little as 6,400 rads can kill most immature cockroaches. A full-grown cockroach would shuffle off this mortal coil on a relatively small blast of 20,000 rads. Wimps! Even the relatively small bomb that destroyed Hiroshima would have killed any cockroach that was loitering around ground zero.

So cockroaches are not the creatures best equipped to survive a nuclear war. Not even close. The toughest radiation survivor is not an insect at all, but a bacterium called *Deinococcus radiodurans* (dubbed Conan the Bacterium by scientists who obviously can't be bothered to take this seriously). This bacterium was discovered in the 1950s growing in rotten, radiation-sprayed meat. It can handle an incredible 1.5 million rads of radiation, and even more when frozen.

All these details should give us some idea of how to deal with the next cockroach plague. Don't try to behead them or starve them, because they'll survive that. Instead, simply launch a nuclear missile at them (there are plenty around) and wipe them off the face of the Earth.

Problem solved.

Plymouth Rock

• • •

The northeastern United States is the place to go for historic sites. If you're ever in Philadelphia, $3 will get you into the Betsy Ross House, where Betsy Ross may have lived (or, as there's no evidence, possibly not). Whether or not it really was her house, it is the best place to find out about the woman who possibly sewed the first American flag (though possibly not) and be greeted by Betsy herself—or at least an actor who looks like her (although, as Ross never posed for any portraits, maybe not).

When I visited the Betsy Ross House, I was aware that this might not have been her house, and she might not have made the flag. Though it felt slightly rude, I couldn't resist asking a young guide about this. The guide sheepishly admitted that there is no real evidence of Betsy's claim to fame, merely circumstantial support (like the fact that Betsy knew George Washington, so she *must* have sewn the flag). "It was considered treason to assist the Revolutionary cause," said the guide, proficiently but somewhat nervously, "so she would have kept quiet about it."

While the Betsy Ross House's claims are suspect, at least it is "an interesting example of the homes of the period" (as described by the state of Pennsylvania). Even if Betsy didn't live there, and didn't make the flag, it wouldn't be America's most overrated tourist site. That would be Plymouth Rock in Massachusetts.

Plymouth is the rock where the pilgrims landed, and on which they were seated, when they arrived in the *Mayflower* in 1620. Plymouth Rock, it has been suggested, signifies the birth of America. "This Rock has become an object of veneration in the United States," wrote Alexis de Tocqueville in 1835. "Here is a stone which the feet of a few outcasts pressed for an instant; and the stone becomes famous; it is treasured by a great nation; its very dust is shared as a relic."

Naturally, the Rock attracts scores of tourists, but with respect, it's a fairly nondescript piece of rock, only of interest because "1620" was engraved into it 260 years later, in 1880. Its modesty wouldn't make it any less historic, of course, unless you start asking questions like "How do we know it's the right rock?" There was no evidence from the original settlers to say that they landed on this rock. The only testimony was from a ninety-four-year-old man, Elder Thomas Faunce, in 1741 (120 years after the event). He claimed that his father had told him the story when he was a boy. The fact that his father had arrived on a later ship, in 1623, might suggest that he really had no idea.

Let's assume for a moment that, through some miracle, this really was the rock on which the Pilgrims landed. It still wouldn't be quite the sacred relic it is claimed to be, because the first English settlement in North America was Jamestown, Virginia, founded thirteen years earlier, and perhaps best known as the place where John Smith was based when he met Pocahontas. This was a trade-based settlement, however. Plymouth was just as significant, as it was the first place where the Pilgrims landed to escape persecution, introducing America as the "land of the free."

Unfortunately, that's not true either. The first place the Pilgrims landed wasn't Plymouth, but Provincetown, on the tip of Cape Cod. Strangely, that's one historic site that nobody seems to know.

Encyclopaedia Britannica

• • •

When French composer Maurice Jarre died in 2009, a Dublin student penned a phony quote and attributed it to Jarre in his entry on the online reference site Wikipedia. ("When I die there will be a final waltz playing in my head that only I can hear," was part of the poetic quote that Jarre never actually said.) Within hours, the quote had made its way into his obituaries on dozens of blogs and newspaper websites. The fraud still hadn't been noticed after a month, so it was left to the student himself to reveal everything.

You've probably heard about how unreliable Wikipedia is. Democracy may be a great thing, but it was always risky allowing anyone with an Internet connection to make anonymous changes and additions to an encyclopedia that receives 2.5 billion page views per month.

Naturally, it's caused plenty of trouble. In the space of a few months in 2005, for example, Norwegian Prime Minister Jens Stoltenberg discovered that his entry had been edited to include libelous statements; a former MTV personality edited himself a bigger role in the history of podcasting (though he said that he was just making it more accurate); and the entry on U.S. journalist John Seigenthaler implicated him in the assassination of President Kennedy—a piece of creative embellishment from someone trying to win a workplace bet.

Another website, Wikipedia Scanner, later traced a few of the editors, like the one at the U.S. Democratic Party headquarters who edited a page on a popular radio announcer, saying that his 20 million listeners were "legally retarded." Other organizations—the CIA, the Vatican, the Republican Party, the United Nations, the Senate—have also made some rather self-serving edits. Considering that Wikipedia has millions of entries, there are probably thousands of other hoaxes that nobody has noticed yet.

The more press the Wikipedia problem gets, the more some of us may wish we could afford to buy (and have shelf space for) a *real* set of encyclopedias, with their leather-bound, multivolume air of authority—particularly the one that held the pre-Internet record as the world's largest encyclopedia: the revered *Encyclopaedia Britannica*. Back in 1929, *Time* magazine dubbed the *Britannica* the "Patriarch of the Library," and naturalist William Beebe was quoted as saying it was "beyond comparison because there is no competitor." (Then again, I got those quotes from Wikipedia, so take them with a grain of salt.) A. J. Jacobs, an editor at *Esquire* magazine, spent a year reading all thirty-two volumes of the 2002 *Britannica* in his quest to become "the smartest person in the world."

Exhaustive as it may have been by that time, *Britannica* has still been obsolete, inaccurate, and incomplete. Harvey Einbender said in his 1964 study *The Myth of the Britannica* that they didn't get it right until the eleventh edition, published in 1910–11.

And still it was far from perfect. Even the 1958 edition had several entries that hadn't changed since the ninth edition, in 1883. Demographics for major Polish cities remained unchanged since 1931, suggesting (among other things) that half the population of Tarnopol was still Jewish. An entry on classical languages still claimed that the study of Latin and Greek was flourishing. "Perhaps this explains," wrote Einbender, "why the entry on Cicero contains eight lines of Latin and the article on Sophocles four lines of Greek without translation." Einbender also somehow had the time (and the brilliance) to find errors in six hundred other entries, including the Old Testament, Homer, Galileo, Napoleon, and Verdi. Not exactly obscure topics.

However confusing this was in 1958, *Britannica* proudly announced that, with its 1961 edition, it had lifted its game. "Before Columbus proved the world was round," ran one advertisement, "people thought the horizon marked its edge . . . Today we know better."

Uh-oh. *Britannica* was still getting it wrong—even before anyone had a chance to read it! Despite the myth (created by early American writers like Washington Irving), almost nobody in Columbus's day thought that the Earth was flat. Plato and Aristotle had told everyone that the Earth was round eighteen hundred years before Columbus was born.

Britannica has ironed out its flaws by now, right? Well, it's hard to say . . . but probably not. Even in 2005, the science journal *Nature* compared the accuracy of science entries in Wikipedia and *Britannica* and found that the difference was "not particularly great: the average science entry in Wikipedia contained around four inaccuracies; *Britannica*, about three." *Britannica* responded that "we in no way mean to imply that *Britannica* is error-free; we have never made such a claim."

Nitpicking? Sure. But a tome that is considered an unquestionable fountain of knowledge should be prepared for malcontents like myself to moan about small things. True, Wikipedia is more troublesome since it's used by more people than any other reference work, but in its defense, it has clamped down on inaccuracies, asking that its contributors provide footnotes for all their facts (and making it clear when they don't). Of course, just because something is footnoted, it doesn't make it true.

And just because an encyclopedia is compiled by a distinguished team of experts and academics (as *Britannica* has been for 240 years), it doesn't mean it's 100 percent reliable.

Sharks

• • •

The shark is probably the most feared animal of them all, scaring people so much that they can barely wade knee-deep into the ocean waters without fear of being dragged down by one of these man-eating monsters. This fear exists in part because when sharks attack, they make the news.

And why do sharks make the news (apart from the fact that gruesome news tends to sell)? Think of the famous line, attributed to New York newspaper editor John Bogart: "When a dog bites a man, that is not news, because it happens so often. But if a man bites a dog, that is news." Ditto if a shark bites a man.

That's not to say that sharks are harmless and cute. Each year, about fifty shark attacks are recorded worldwide. Of those, about one-fifth are fatal. Australia, notorious for its fatal shark attacks, has had only fifty-six in the past fifty years. Yes, despite the shark-infested seas of Sydney and Perth, Aussie sharks probably won't kill you. You have eight times more chance of dying in a scuba-diving accident, three hundred times more chance of drowning, and two thousand times more chance of dying in a car accident. You even have nearly twice as much chance of dying from bee stings or from being struck by lightning.

If you insist on being attacked by a shark, it's best to stay in America. In the past five hundred years, there have been more than one thousand shark attacks in the United States (mostly in Hawaii), but less than a hundred of them have been fatal. See? Not so bad, really.

Even if you are swimming in open water and come across a school of sharks, there is probably no reason to panic. There are about 350 species of sharks, and only thirty of them are known to attack humans. They might be mean-looking critters, but they aren't the vicious maniacs that their reputation might suggest. If you really want to boast to your friends that you were mauled by a shark, the best thing to do (apart from having your head examined) is to blunder into their territory and throw yourself out of your boat, so you can be perceived as a threat. If the shark still doesn't attack, you can pull its tail or try to hand-feed it, as some dim-witted divers have been known to do.

If a shark is approaching, you can still defend yourself by hitting its eyes or gills with your fists, your legs, your handbag (if you go scuba diving with your handbag), a conveniently placed softball bat, or whatever else you have. This will show that you're no easy catch, and the shark will likely turn around and leave you alone. How wimpy is that?

Sharks, like most animals, eat to survive. They don't

have human intelligence, hence they won't attack you in a fit of malice. But what if they were as smart as humans? This was the conceit behind one shark movie, *Deep Blue Sea* (1999), in which a team of scientists get some especially fierce sharks and make them super-smart. The newly intelligent sharks cause no end of trouble, gruesomely killing six people before they are outwitted by LL Cool J and Thomas Jane (suggesting that they couldn't have been so smart after all).

Why would sharks be so vicious? Well, if they had human-level intelligence, they might attack humans out of revenge—and they'd be justified. The number of humans killed by sharks each year may not reach double figures, but humans eat tens of millions of sharks. You may not think you've ever tried shark meat, but it's called flake or white fillet and is fairly common at seafood bars. Then there's that Oriental delicacy called shark fin soup, for which fishermen catch the sharks in a net, slice off their fins, and throw the finless sharks back in the water, where, unable to swim, they bleed to death. But sharks have such a bad reputation that you might think it's just as well that fishermen are killing them, helping to rid the world of the scourge of the sea, rather than destroying an essential part of the ecosystem.

Some of the most unexpected people have leapt to the defense of sharks in recent years, including the late Peter Benchley. Toward the end of his life, Benchley became a strong advocate for the conservation of sharks—which was the least he could do, because he wrote the novel *Jaws*, about a malevolent great white shark. As this bestseller was turned into one of the biggest box office movies in history, Benchley probably did more than anyone to make us hate and fear sharks.

Happily, Benchley wasn't the only one trying to turn the reputation of sharks around. In the coastal city of Baltimore, one of the hotels employs "Mr. Bite," a friendly shark (or to be more accurate, a guy in a cuddly Barney-like shark costume), who entertains the kids at breakfast. Presumably, he's supposed to encourage them to hug the next shark they see. Of course, he could use a name change.

Whatever you do, go and enjoy a swim at the beach, safe in the knowledge that you have practically no chance of being carried away by an angry shark. If you must have a terrible fear of any animal, may I suggest the humble mosquito? These troublemakers have killed several *billion* people over the centuries. Happily, medical technology means that, in the Western world at least, we are now far less likely to catch a fatal dose of malaria, yellow fever, dengue fever, or any number of other diseases from these pests. Still, they're a lot more dangerous than sharks.

The Renaissance

◆ ◆ ◆

Perhaps no time in history is revered as much as the Renaissance, that period of about two hundred years just following the Middle Ages, renowned for its cultural and intellectual advances (in Europe, at least). Indeed, the word "renaissance" (French for "rebirth") is now used to describe any sort of blossoming of arts or culture, especially if it follows a bleak period. But none of these "renaissances" are on par with *the* Renaissance. Who can argue that any era that gave us a blossoming of learning, and the genius of Giotto, Michelangelo, Shakespeare, Bacon, Dante, Brunelleschi, Donatello, and many others, wasn't touched by greatness?

Nobody seems to agree about exactly when the Renaissance started. All we know is that by the mid-fifteenth century, the Italian writer Matteo Palmieri could suggest that every man "thank God that it has been permitted to him to be born in this new age, so full of hope and promise," and architect Antonio Filarete could look back on the Dark Ages as a time when "learning was lacking in Italy," until the miraculous day when "men's minds were sharpened and awakened" (whatever day that was).

Despite a few setbacks, humanity has progressed continuously over the years. Renaissance scholars were simply among the first to notice. The Renaissance wasn't so much a magical era when everything suddenly improved, as it was a time when (partly because people started celebrating humanity rather than God) everyone was rather full of themselves and, like the baby boomers five hundred years later, proud to be born at the "right" time.

Actually, the Dark Ages' bad rap was always a little unfair: "dark ages" and "medieval" are generally not complimentary things to say about anything. Sure, the Dark Ages gave us the Crusades, hideous plagues, and shocking amounts of religious persecution, but you could also say that about the past seventy-five years. The Dark Ages also gave us the birth of modern chemistry, Gothic architecture, and the nautical compass. Aristotle was rediscovered with the translations of Muslim philosopher Ibn-Rushd, and the first universities were established, including Oxford. Indeed, the term "Dark Ages" is deemed so unfair that most historians now prefer the term "Middle Ages."

Just like the Renaissance, the Middle Ages was a time of progress. Living standards rose, with major advances in technology, medical science, and (oh yes!) the arts. As the era drew to a close, however, Europe was like a fourteenth-century Bangladesh, suffering from widespread famine and, most notably, the Black Plague, which is thought to have killed at least a third of Europe's population. Progress effectively stalled.

Then came the Renaissance, and Europe seemed to rise again from the ashes. Unfortunately, in every era you have to take the rough with the smooth. The Renaissance may have been the time that European civilization took over the world—a mixed blessing—but the water was still dirty, disease was still rampant, monarchs were still cruel, and codpieces were a fashion accessory. It wasn't the time travelers' utopia that some of Europe's historians would have you believe. In fact, parts of it were downright "medieval." Among them:

Witch Hunts

While the people of the Dark Ages believed in witchcraft, they stopped short of actually executing any witches. It wasn't until the Renaissance that such unfortunate women were put to death in the hundreds of thousands. So much for enlightened beliefs . . .

The Spanish Inquisition

Some twenty-five thousand people were executed (and many others tortured) for heresy in one of the most shameful moments in the history of the Catholic Church and of Spain. (True, twenty-five thousand is a small number compared to many other dark episodes in history, but it was still a hideous time.)

Vicious Conquerors

As Europe began to colonize the world, the pioneers took a leaf from the Vandals, the Barbarians, the Visigoths, and any other notorious invaders you may care to name. In the New World, explorers like Columbus, Pizarro, and Cortés were vicious despots, mercilessly wiping out thriving civilizations with such superior weapons as firearms and exotic diseases.

Destroying the Past

While Renaissance scholars revered the ancient world, Renaissance developers had no sense of preservation. The majesty of ancient Rome, still standing after many centuries, was demolished to make way for modern architecture. Even St. Peter's Basilica, "the oldest, most sacred building in Christendom," was toppled after twelve hundred years. Thousands of ancient marble statues were melted down to make lime. Meanwhile, gems of medieval architecture, such as the Notre Dame Cathedral in Paris, were left to fall apart until centuries later, when movements were formed to restore them. While some (like Michelangelo) protested at this super-vandalism, other denizens of the Renaissance were content to destroy the past.

Coffee Ban

As the brew seemed to stimulate radical thought, coffee was banned in Mecca in 1511, meaning that devoted coffee drinkers had to do without. Okay, it's not as bad as the Spanish Inquisition, but it sounds like sheer torture!

∞∞∞∞∞∞∞∞∞∞∞∞∞∞∞∞∞∞∞∞∞∞∞∞∞∞∞∞∞∞∞∞∞∞

Why the World Was Doing Fine Before the Renaissance, Thank You Very Much

The Renaissance was labeled by an eighteenth-century European historian. Europe ruled the waves by then, and European history was the only history that seemed to matter. We've had a similar attitude ever since, but the Renaissance was merely centered in Europe (and most of the time, just Italy). The pre-Renaissance world was actually flourishing.

In fact, if anyone was sitting around in the Dark Ages moaning, "Nothing happens around here," chances are they were in Europe. They would have simply needed to walk across the Sahara for several months to find the West African empire of Mali, one of the world's largest empires, with Timbuktu established as the center of Islamic schooling. Otherwise, the traveler could sail across the Atlantic (as Cortés and Pizarro eventually did) to see the marvels of the New World—including the spectacular Aztec city of Tenochtitlan (population: 250,000).

The achievements of these civilizations are even more astonishing than their fates; Mali is now one of the world's poorest nations, but at least it's fared better than Tenochtitlan (RIP).

Meanwhile, in Asia, Cambodia's Angkor Wat, the world largest religious monument, was completed around 1150. Japan boasted the world's largest city (or would have done so, if it were a boastful culture). This was Edo (now known as Tokyo), part of a thriving civilization of 30 million people.

But the world's largest empire was the Chinese empire, with a population of 120 million, the "Great" Wall, the Forbidden City, and huge textile, porcelain, and paper industries. This was the civilization revealed in the thirteenth century to that wonderstruck Italian explorer, Marco Polo.

◇◇

The QWERTY Keyboard

• • •

When I first saw my dad using a typewriter (back when I was very small, in the days before word processors), I was fascinated by how fast he could type, how he could do it without even looking at the keyboard, and most of all, why the letters were in such a strange order. "The people who designed typewriters worked out that it's easier that way," he explained, "based on the letters that are most commonly used."

The lesson: don't believe everything your parents tell you. In this case, Dad was mistaken. In fact, the QWERTY keyboard (named for the first six keys in the upper row of letters, for those who have been in Siberia for the past thirty years) was designed to make typing *more* difficult and *slow us down*. Yes, seriously!

When the first typewriter was built in 1867, by Milwaukee publisher Christopher Sholes and his partners, the letters were arranged in alphabetical order. This would have made more sense to my young eyes, but this model was somewhat crude. If you got carried away and typed too fast (which didn't need to be very fast at all), the letters could jam at the roller. (Sorry for all this tech talk, for those too young to know what a "roller" is.)

To slow down any overexcited typist, James Densmore, one of Sholes's co-inventors, asked his son-in-law (a school superintendent) what letters and combinations of letters appeared most often in the English language. In 1872, Densmore and Sholes devised a keyboard that placed what they believed to be the most used characters as far apart as possible on the keyboard. So was born QWERTY.

Following a few design innovations, it didn't take long for the action of typewriters to become smooth enough to make such a system obsolete. There have been many attempts to improve on it, most notably by educational psychologist August Dvorak, who in 1932 invented the Dvorak Simplified Keyboard, or DSK—or, to name it after the first six keys (à la QWERTY), the PYFGCR keyboard. No, sorry, let's just go with DSK.

Dvorak's keyboard was the result of twenty years of research, in which he studied thousands of words to discover the most common letters and combinations. One of his first conclusions: you had a good chance of devising a better keyboard than QWERTY simply by arranging the letters at random. (This would have been good news for Sholes and Densmore, as that was the whole reason they invented their ungainly system.) Using the DSK, 70 percent of a typist's work (including all the vowels) can be done in the middle row, 22 percent in the row above and 8 percent below. The work is focused on the right hand, but a version for left-handed people was also devised.

So how much better was the DSK model? Dvorak demonstrated it in the coolest way: he took it out on the sports field. Back in the 1930s, typing competitions were all the rage. (Who says people didn't know how to have fun back then?) DSK keyboards were like the typing equivalent of polyurethane swimsuits, or the original Nike Air Pegasus running shoe, except better. It produced several champions, including Lenore MacClain, one of Dvorak's students at the University of Washington, whose QWERTY speed was 70 words a minute. Switched to DSK, she was typing up to 182 words a minute. The Jesse Owens of her sport, she broke eight world records in typing and transcription. While she was obviously outstanding, many other DSK typists doubled their speeds, breaking the 100-words-a-minute barrier. The current (and long-term) speed record is held by Barbara Blackburn, who would go to each secretarial job with her personal DSK typewriter under her arm. She achieved a peak speed of 212 words per minute.

The DSK was also easier to learn, as Dvorak proved during World War II, retraining fourteen women in the U.S. Navy to use his keyboard. After only a month, they were churning out 74 percent more work and were 68 percent more accurate. It was considerably more economical than the QWERTY keyboard as well.

For those who really like sports statistics: with DSK, a typist's fingertips only needed to move about one mile on an average day, compared with twelve to twenty miles a day with a QWERTY keyboard. Great news for sufferers of the then-unnamed repetitive strain injury (RSI). After several more tests over the years, the U.S. Bureau of Standards finally said in 1965 that there was "little need to demonstrate further the superiority of the Dvorak keyboard in experimental tests. Plenty of well-documented evidence exists."

So if it's that good, why don't we use it? While it would be fun to suggest a sinister conspiracy theory, the truth is that nobody stands to gain much from the continuing use of QWERTY. It was different when the DSK was released; converting a typewriter keyboard back then was a heck of a soldering job. But now, laptops (both Mac and PC) are available with the Dvorak layout, and software is available to transform your keyboard to DSK.

So what's our excuse now? Just that most of us learned to type on the standard keyboard, and I can't see many people (including myself) making the transition for some time. It would be tougher than converting to the metric system. We'll just make do with the clunky, less efficient model that we know so well.

The Jazz Singer

• • •

*T*he *Jazz Singer* is one of those very famous movies from the early years of cinema—like *The Great Train Robbery* or *Battleship Potemkin*—that nobody seems to have actually seen. That wasn't the case when it was first released in 1927. It was the sort of movie that Hollywood publicists would in later years describe as a "mega-hit," costing $500,000 to make and earning a profit of $3 million (a lot of money in those days).

Most of the people who flocked to see it are now dead, but its reputation lingers on. *The Jazz Singer* was the first "talkie" (movie with sound), changing the movies from silent to "all-singing, all-dancing" (or at least, all-sound). It was a milestone. During the 1920s, many people were staying at home to listen to the latest gadget, the radio, with all the excitement of live broadcasts, audio plays, and the latest hit songs. *The Jazz Singer* saved Warner Bros. Pictures from bankruptcy, and may have saved the movie business as well.

This was an impressive role in history for any movie to play. But as with so many other things in Hollywood, it's mostly hype. *The Jazz Singer* was not the first talkie. In fact, strictly speaking, it wasn't even a talkie.

It was not as though the Warner brothers were the first people to ever think of talking pictures. Thomas Edison and his team of overworked and underpaid, but brilliant, technicians had considered the idea when they first marketed moving pictures in the late nineteenth century. Edison even equipped some of his early peep-show machines with phonographs, which he called "Kineto-phones," to play sound along with the movie, but they were usually out of sync.

Studios and inventors experimented with synchronized sound for the next thirty years. In August 1926, the Warners released *Don Juan*, their first feature film to test the Vitaphone process, starring one of their top actors, the dashing John Barrymore. The focus was on the score (not by Liszt, who wrote the opera, but by Hollywood composer William Axt) and sound effects. Thanks to Vitaphone, it opened in theaters with some short musical films.

Though *Don Juan* isn't as famous now as *The Jazz Singer*, that doesn't mean it wasn't popular. The program, made up of shorts and the feature, was a smashing success. It played in New York for well more than six months. Still, you could get the idea that Warner Bros. was near bankruptcy in 1926 simply by misinterpreting the annual accounts. Between 1925 and 1926, they went from a $1.1 million profit to a $1.3 million loss. This sounds pretty shocking, until you realize that they were investing in talking pictures. In all, they would spend $5 million developing this technology—considerably more than *The Jazz Singer* ever made.

But while *Don Juan* had proven that Vitaphone could work with feature films, they still hadn't tried one thing: dialogue. So was this the big innovation of *The Jazz Singer*?

Well . . . no. In January 1927, rival Fox Studios (using a rival sound system, Movietone) was already making short talkies. By the time *The Jazz Singer* came in October, talkies were practically old news.

Yet *The Jazz Singer* was still basically a silent film (played in cinemas with piano accompaniment, like other silent films), with just a few moments of synchronized sound. How uncool was that! The sound was mainly just a few opportunities for the title character, played by veteran theater superstar Al Jolson, to sing songs like "Blue Skies" and "My Mammy" (which were oldies even back then). Yes, there was dialogue, but each line was ad-libbed by Jolson and Eugenie Besserer (who played his mother—sorry, his "mammy"). Jolson spoke a grand total of 281 words in the film.

It wasn't until 1928 that Warner Bros. made their first film with scripted dialogue, *Tenderloin*, and their first "all-talking" film, *The Lights of New York*. They also made *The Singing Fool*, an all-talkie follow-up to *The Jazz Singer*, which was considerably more popular (at the time, the most popular film they had ever made). It even featured a new song, "Sonny Boy" (written by the popular team of De Sylva, Brown, and Henderson), which was a far bigger hit than anything in *The Jazz Singer*.

So *The Jazz Singer* just hinted at the potential of talkies, without actually being one. "You ain't heard nothin' yet!" says Jolson, in his most famous line of (improvised) dialogue. True enough. The audiences had heard close to nothing.

The Grand Canyon

◆ ◆ ◆

We've all heard about the Seven Wonders of the Ancient World, a checklist of the must-see attractions (in the Western world, at least) allegedly chosen by the Greek poet Antipater of Sidon in the first century BC. If Antipater was indeed responsible for this list, he has a claim to fame that today's travel writers must envy. Despite his limited knowledge of "the world" (the wonders of Asia and the Americas had not yet been discovered by the Greeks), everyone seems to regard his list as the official record, and his sole authority has rarely been questioned. When the Seven Wonders of the Modern World were announced in 2007 by the Switzerland-based New7Wonders Foundation, literally millions of votes were cast, but everyone *still* disagreed with it.

There are too many candidates, of course. But what

is the most *overrated* wonder of the world? Not just including the New Seven Wonders list, but every mountain, monument, building, natural formation, structure, monolith, forest, waterfall, amusement park, and tourist attraction that you can name? Using my sole, Antipater-like wisdom, I have to say that the winner is . . . the Grand Canyon in Arizona.

To which many proud American readers would say: "What would you know, you Australian nitwit? I wasn't too impressed by the Great Barrier Reef or the Sydney Opera House, *so there*!" Granted, the Grand Canyon is a spectacular site, easily the deepest canyon to be carved over millions of years by the mighty Colorado River. It is truly awesome, so including it in this book is just plain rude. However, this chapter can also be named "Attractions That Are Supposed to Be the Greatest in the World, But Aren't."

At its deepest, the Grand Canyon drops 5,700 feet from canyon rim to water. This is nothing compared to Hell's Canyon in Idaho, cut by the Snake River. It isn't as wide as Arizona's greatest attraction, but it's much deeper. Running east from the Seven Devils Mountain, the valley floor drops 7,900 feet—2,200 feet deeper than the Grand Canyon at its deepest.

Travelers are always impressed by any structure or natural wonder that is known as the world's largest. They would go to Haskovo in Bulgaria if they knew it had the largest statue of the Virgin Mary, looking down on them from 46 feet. They will go to Quebec to see the world's largest self-supporting igloo, with an internal height of 12.5 feet. They will even travel to Australia's Sunshine Coast to see the 52-foot-high Big Pineapple, which isn't even a real pineapple.

Other "big" sites, however, are merely hype. Just so that

no Arizonans think I'm picking on them, here are a few other Wonders of the World that aren't as big, deep, or high as they are renowned to be:

The Great Pyramid of Cheops

One of Antipater's original Seven Wonders, this feat of engineering was nothing short of miraculous when it was built around 2600 BC, a good two thousand years before any of the other ancient wonders were built. Since the fifteenth century, when the Tomb of Mausolus in Turkey was disassembled by Crusaders, the Great Pyramid has been all that remained from Antipater's list.

But as well as being one of the world's most incredible structures, the Great Pyramid is usually considered the world's biggest pyramid. It is certainly the largest in Egypt, but it isn't as large as some of the pre-Columbian pyramids in Mexico, probably built for the Aztec and Toltec gods more than two thousand years ago. The base of Quetzalcoatl, in Cholula de Rivadabia, takes up forty-five acres, and the pyramid itself contains 4.3 million cubic yards of material. The Great Pyramid takes up a relatively modest 13 acres and 3.4 million cubic yards of stone. Quetzalcoatl is easily the largest pyramid.

In fact, Cheops's pyramid doesn't even come second. Another Mexican pyramid, Teotihuacan (the Pyramid of the Sun), has a circumference of 2,800 feet at its base. Okay, so the Great Pyramid is still 433 feet tall, which is more than twice as high as Teotihuacan. Also, though larger that the Great Pyramid, the pyramids of Mexico are not such marvels of geometric engineering, being constructed imprecisely with steps and layers. As a result, the

Great Pyramid might still be the *greatest* pyramid. Just not as big.

Uluru

Australians proudly claim to have the world's largest monolith—and they're right. The only thing is, it isn't Uluru (formerly Ayers Rock), as most people (including Aussies) believe. It is in fact Burringurrah, or Mount Augustus, located in a remote area of Western Australia. Burringurrah rises 2,815 feet over the ground, with a ridge five miles long. Uluru, in comparison, rises a mere 1,099 feet above the plain (though it's more than five miles in circumference). Uluru wouldn't win the "world's largest monolith" title anyway, simply because it's not a monolith, but part of a huge underground rock formation.

Mount Everest

One of the easiest trivia questions in the world, asked in kids' quiz games between "What's the capital of England?" and "Who sang 'Womanizer'?" is "What is the world's highest mountain?" The real answer: Well, it depends. The famous Mount Everest, at 29,000 feet, is the world's highest mountain above sea level, but not the highest point on Earth. Mount Chimborazo in Ecuador is 7,224 feet farther from the center of the Earth. Then there's Mauna Kea in Hawaii. When measured from seabed to summit, it's 33,464 feet high—more than half a mile higher than Everest.

But that's just nitpicking.

The Magna Carta

◆ ◆ ◆

Every British schoolboy (and many a schoolboy outside Britain) knows that, when the dastardly King John of England was forced to sign the Magna Carta in Runnymede in 1215, he—and his successors—could no longer ride roughshod over their subjects. To this day, the Magna Carta is a document equated with lawfulness, freedom, and democracy. Radical politician John Wilkes, in 1763, called it "that glorious inheritance, that distinguishing characteristic of the Englishmen." At the time, ironically, he was imprisoned for sedition in the Tower of London.

The document is celebrated in England, but revered even more in the United States, where many consider it a forebear to the Declaration of Independence. This all sounds very nice, but they might not realize that Thomas Jefferson's statement in the Declaration that "all men are created equal" (an ideal he described as "self-evident") was far more innovative and audacious than most people today would imagine. The Magna Carta was a great one for personal rights and freedoms, *provided you were a nobleman*. (Noble*women*? Forget it!) If you were one of the three-quarters of the population who were not wealthy, and toiled your life away for the landowners, the document wasn't really of much use to you.

When the barons of England wrote the Magna Carta, they were motivated not by a sense of great injustice, but by their sense of outrage when King John tried to increase their rental fees. John's numerous acts of cruelty and murder, even his cowardly evacuation from the battlefield at Normandy (leaving his soldiers to die), might have been good reasons to take action, but in the end, it was all down to rent. The charter did provide for a committee of barons to supervise the king, but as the barons were notoriously ruthless, this was no great improvement.

The barons celebrated the Magna Carta because of the new rights that they had won, but even for them it needed work. Under the original charter, trial by combat and trial by ordeal (in which the accused could prove his innocence by bathing in boiling tar) were perfectly legal. Fortunately, the document later was given a few necessary tweaks. Most significantly, in 1369, Edward III replaced the words "no free man" with the language "no man, of whatever estate or condition he may be" and added that nobody could be dispossessed, imprisoned, or executed without "due process of law."

Still, it wasn't a magic document that brought joy and fairness to the world. John had always hoped that it would be a toothless symbol of his generosity, and it wasn't much better than that. Though it was supposed to curtail the power of the English monarchy, England had some of its most tyrannical monarchs after John's death. Henry VIII was perhaps the most famous example, frequently violating his subjects' rights as he forced them to join his new church. Throughout all of this, the upper classes rarely said, "Now hold on a doggone minute, Your Majesty, don't forget the Magna Carta!" They saw the document as a protector of their property, and no more. (Besides, they wouldn't have said words like "doggone.")

You can blame political propaganda for the Magna Carta's great reputation. A seventeenth-century lord chief justice, Sir Edward Coke, revealed the previously obscure document to Parliament as part of a chain of royal confirmations of English law, dating as far back as 1042. He may have played loose with the facts, but his "discovery" did help to inspire the English Civil Wars of 1642–48, which led to the first Commonwealth of England. Coke's revisionist history of England, with its ceaseless advance of liberty and freedom, was later dismissed as a political stunt. Royalist writers, meanwhile, saw the Magna Carta as an irrelevant feudal document. They may have been right, but the Coke version—far more inspiring—took hold. In Victorian Britain, it was used to justify Britannia's rule over a colonial empire, as it showed Britain as a model for other freedom-loving nations. (This presumably included India, whose subjects were fighting to free themselves from the yoke of the British Empire, and the United States, which was still trying to end the Britain-inherited practice of slavery.)

The Magna Carta is now most useful as a symbolic moment of history, with the nobles as the good guys (which is hard to take seriously) and bad, evil, wicked, vicious, disgraceful, et cetera, King John as the villain (which is easier to take seriously). Incidentally, whatever you may have seen in paintings or old movies, John did *not* sign away his rights to be an appalling tyrant and exploit his subjects. In fact, he may have been illiterate. As a look at any of the "original" copies would reveal (there are seventeen of them, dating from 1297 or earlier), he simply placed his Royal Seal upon it.

Spinach

· · ·

Spinach is good for you—and more flavorsome than many other green vegetables (which are also good for you)—so just because spinach is in this book, there's no reason not to eat it. However, the idea that it imparts almost superhuman strength is not so true. So why have so many parents ordered their children to eat their spinach, insisting that it would give them great muscles? It should really be one of the greatest health scandals of all time, and it's all the fault of a stray decimal point.

In 1870, German scientist Dr. E. von Wolf discovered that spinach contains iron, an essential vitamin in building physical strength. When scribbling down the results, however, he misplaced the decimal point, thereby making it official that spinach had ten times more iron (as much as meat!) than it actually did. It would be decades before these figures were rechecked.

In the meantime, spinach seemed like an ideal food to the U.S. government. During the Great Depression (and later, World War II rationing), it was promoted as an excellent meat substitute. To help them spread the word, the government hired one of America's favorite celebrities: Popeye the sailor man.

Popeye, renowned for getting into fights and mangling the English language, was introduced in 1929 as a supporting character in Elzie Crisler Segar's comic strip *Thimble Theatre*. He was so popular that he eventually took over from the strip's original heroes, Harold Ham Gravy and Castor Oyl. (Castor went into comic-strip limbo, while Popeye took his sister Olive—and seventy-five years later, after one of the longest courtships in literary history, finally married the woman.) By 1940, he was probably America's most popular comic strip character.

As one of the great ruffians of the comic-strip page, Popeye was an ideal choice to advertise the strength-giving properties of spinach. From that moment on, the secret of his superhuman strength was revealed. In his comics and (more dramatically) his cinema cartoons, whenever he seemed on the verge of losing a fight, he squeezed open a tin of spinach (using the kind of brute strength that suggested that he didn't really need any help), poured the spinach down his throat, and pummeled his opponent, to the triumphant strains of his theme tune.

Soon after Popeye took up spinach, sales of spinach in the United States increased by a third. Among American children in the 1930s, spinach became the most popular food after turkey and ice cream. Proof of the power of mass entertainment. The sailor advertised not only spinach but also the merits of a relatively new technology: canned food. Those who have seen any of the hundreds of short Popeye cartoons (dating back to 1932) will have noticed that Popeye never consumed any fresh spinach, but only the tinned variety. At the time, cans were a perfect way to stock up on emergency food supplies.

But just as tins are never as easy to open as Popeye made it look, getting such strength from a can of spinach is not so easy either. It was not until the 1930s that the truth about the stray decimal point was known. By then, the damage had been done. Generations of parents have now tortured their children by making them eat their spinach so they could be "big and strong, just like Popeye."

For the record, half a cup of cooked spinach contains 1.4 mg of iron. Alternatively, half a cup of cooked pumpkin has 1.7 mg, two tablespoons of molasses have 3.6 mg, half a cup of tofu has 6.7 mg, and, for Popeye-level strength, a quarter of a cup of roasted pumpkin seeds will provide 8.5 mg of iron. These are all sources of nonheme iron (which make them useful for vegetarians), but if you really want to make sure you get your iron, a medical expert might suggest that you eat plenty of boiled cockles, black pudding, liver, and kidney. It seems that to get strength, you'll need a strong stomach.

Okay, spinach does have some iron. But then, it also has oxalic acid, which binds with iron, inhibiting its absorption in the body. So if you want to eat spinach, you should balance it with other foods (especially vitamin C–rich foods, like broccoli, Brussels sprouts, tomato, potato, fish, and poultry) that absorb the iron. Dietary science isn't as easy as Popeye made it look.

But spinach isn't all bad. At least it has enough beta carotene to be good for your night vision. Slightly more than carrots, at least.

Ulysses by James Joyce

• • •

As I mentioned in the introduction, I tried to avoid art criticism in this list of the most overrated things in history. Connoisseurs have suggested to me that Mozart's *Magic Flute*, say, or Van Gogh's *Sunflowers* were vastly overrated (and of course, I can name a few great works of art that don't impress me as much as they impressed other people). But this is not meant to be a book of critique. Even the works of art that made the list (like *Titanic* and *Sgt. Pepper's Lonely Hearts Club Band*) did so for reasons other than their artistry (or lack thereof).

Yet I couldn't help thinking of James Joyce's 1922 novel *Ulysses*. Like many people, I was unmoved by this book, but I'd never read the many analyses and academic tomes devoted to it, so I could accept that perhaps I didn't understand or appreciate it for the work of genius it truly is—and that my ignorance was the reason I found it te-dious and unreadable.

For that reason, I didn't feel qualified to include *Ulysses* in this book. A friend, however, reminded me that I've been a book reviewer and a "literary scholar" (whatever that means), so I was qualified to write about whatever book I wanted. Hey, what else would qualify someone to tear apart a book (literally or otherwise)? This gave me pause for thought, after which I decided that I can con-fidently pronounce *Ulysses* the most overrated novel in history.

For the uninitiated (which is most people), *Ulysses* is a book in which a man, Leopold Bloom, walks around Dublin for a day (June 16, 1904). Sometimes he is joined by Stephen Dedalus, a young schoolteacher with liter-ary aspirations. They don't do a great deal else. Stephen teaches English to some kids, he and Leopold go to a brothel (but don't actually use the services, so that's probably not the good bit), they witness a burial, and they have a few meditations on life. Somehow, this takes 932 pages.

Unreadable? Let's just say that the longest sentence con-tains 4,391 words. Joyce might have known all about "stream of consciousness" writing, but he didn't know much about editing. (The sentence held the record until 2001, when Jonathan Coe's *Rotters' Club* gave the literary world a 13,955-word sentence. You probably haven't read that one.) Strangely, Joyce's long sentence has a few para-graph breaks, where—if he bothered with punctuation—he could have simply started a new sentence. The "sentence" is just a long passage without full stops (or, for that matter, commas and apostrophes). But it did give him the dubious record of "longest sentence," presumably to get everyone's attention. (More on that later.)

The book also has humor, in the form of some of the most appalling puns ever written. ("Come forth, Lazarus! And he came fifth, and lost the job." Joyce was a regular Groucho Marx.)

Ulysses has been analyzed beyond all means, probably because it raises so many questions. Why, for example, did someone as smart as James Joyce see fit to use such bad punctuation? And more important, what does it all mean? "I've put in so many enigmas and puzzles that it will keep the professors busy for centuries arguing over what I meant, and that's the only way of ensuring one's immortality," said Joyce of his book. (Actually, writing a few excellent books—or at least a few readable ones—could also help.)

He isn't the only person who wrote to confuse academics. As I mentioned in a previous entry, John Lennon wrote the nonsensical lyrics to "I Am the Walrus" as a joke on the academics who had written him off as a hopeless case at school and now spent their time analyzing his lyrics. But while Lennon did it to be a smart aleck, Joyce did it to be a pretentious git. He admitted as much (sort of). "The demand that I make of my reader is that he should devote his whole life to reading my books," he said.

In case anyone felt like criticizing him, he had an even more obnoxious line: "A man of genius makes no mistakes. His errors are volitional and are the portals of discovery." Despite this, Irish novelist Roddy Doyle (*The Commitments*) confessed in 2004 that he found *Ulysses* "overlong, overrated and unmoving," claiming that it "could have done with a good editor." Even *Mental Floss* magazine named it the world's most overrated work of literature, saying, "We're convinced only eleven people in all of human history have actually read it."

"I have just finished reading the novel *Ulysses* by James Joyce," wrote Australian author Mark Dapin. "It was my third attempt to get through the book, and it took me fifteen months. By comparison, I wrote my own novel, from start to finish, in four months. This proves it's easier to write your own novel than to read *Ulysses*. For anyone who has not read *Ulysses* but has wondered what happens in the book, here is a plot spoiler for you: nothing."

But it was also named the Greatest Novel of the Twentieth Century by the Modern Language Association, and ranked highly in many other "great novel" lists. So why is it so highly rated? Apart from the pretension (of both Joyce and his devotees), a few things come to mind:

- It's widely regarded as an amazing stream-of-consciousness work—although, as it took seven years to write, it might not be as "stream-of-consciousness" as it's supposed to be.

- Its attention to detail is remarkable, capturing Dublin so well that travelers could retrace Bloom's steps through the town. (Not bad considering it was mainly written while Joyce was living in Zurich and Trieste. He had a good memory—I'll give him that.) Then again, I've read a few travelogues that gave equally vivid descriptions of towns and places, and most of them are not considered essential classics in the literary canon.

♦ In America, it was banned for twelve years, which usually helps to raise a book's reputation beyond all measure. When U.S. courts declared it obscene and indecent (read: "we don't understand it"), copies were smuggled from the UK, giving it a cult following in the literary underworld.

♦ The day on which it all takes place, June 16, is now the date of a tourist festival called Bloomsday, celebrated in at least sixty countries, but especially in Dublin, where hundreds of people follow Bloom's route through the city, accompanied by drinking and dramatic reading. It's a much quicker journey than actually reading the book. Government officials lavish praise on *Ulysses*, knowing how much it helps the tourist industry.

♦ If your title is from classical mythology, it always adds intellectual class. Named after the hero of Homer's *Odyssey*, it's considered a perverse, modern-day version of Homer's epic. Note that the major supporting character, Stephen Dedalus, almost shares his name with another figure of Greek myth, Daedalus, the inventor who made Icarus his wings . . . and didn't have a great deal to do with the events of the *Odyssey*.

♦ It's often called "influential," even though, we can probably assume, most literature since then was written by authors who have never read any James Joyce. (You can tell by the way they can string a proper sentence together.) Still, it possibly inspired such stream-of-consciousness epics as Jack Kerouac's almost-as-uneventful *On the Road*, which is, like, totally cool (man). Then again, that might have just been drugs.

Sliced Bread

◆ ◆ ◆

When baker Otto Frederick Rohwedder revealed his mechanical bread slicer in 1928, little did he know the significance of his invention: it would give rise to one of the most enduring and downright annoying phrases in the English language. When anything new and exciting (of any description) is unveiled, someone is bound to call it "the best thing since sliced bread."

Okay, let's put this into perspective. In the years since 1928, the world has been blessed with penicillin, transistors, regular jet travel, satellite technology, solar power, laser surgery, YouTube, and KT Tunstall music, to name but a few great developments in the progress of humanity. Surely something in the past eighty years has transcended even the lofty heights of sliced bread!

In fact, when Rohwedder unveiled his invention, it was regarded with general indifference—which is fair enough.

As generations of single men can tell you, bread is the easiest, laziest food to prepare as it is. Simply slice off a piece from the loaf—an act that takes just a few seconds—and spread something on it. (Jam or butter; they didn't have Nutella back then.) Instant snack! Rather than simplifying, say, veal cordon bleu or asparagus roulade, Rohwedder's bread-slicer further simplified one of the few types of food that seriously didn't need simplifying. How lazy can people get?

Rohwedder himself was anything but lazy. He had spent fifteen years inventing this machine, which seems like a remarkably diligent way to waste time. Fortunately for him, all his hard work was not in vain. Sliced bread eventually became popular, bought by people seemingly oblivious to the way that each slice went stale more quickly than regular bread. Still, this bread was a perfect size for the toaster. Its true worth was discovered in World War II, however, when it took away one of the chores of military caterers providing peanut butter and jelly sandwiches as part of the soldiers' rations in the U.S. Army. (In fact, the peculiar-but-tasty mixture of peanut butter and jelly was almost unknown before the war, and the caterers probably only did it to provide nutritional balance. After the war, the returned servicemen couldn't rid themselves of their addiction.)

So yes, pointless though it might have seemed to Rohwedder's customers back in 1928, sliced bread has had its uses, all leading to that hackneyed line of praise. But as the model for excellence, the model by which everything else is measured, perhaps it should be replaced by something else. How about those pull-apart loaves, especially the ones laced with cheese and spinach? They are surely the best thing since . . . well, since penicillin.

The Trojan War

• • •

Homer's *Iliad*, possibly the first great masterpiece of Western literature, had everything—heroism, power, romance (didn't it all start with the abduction of Helen of Troy, "the face that launched a thousand ships"?). It was great, except for one major flaw: the ending. That's the one where the Greek soldiers fooled their opponents by hiding in a huge wooden horse, which the Trojans duly took behind the walls of their city. Once inside, the Greek warriors pounced on the unsuspecting Trojans.

Sure, it was set a long time ago (in the eighth or ninth century BC), but was anyone in history *ever* that dumb? The Trojans may have been inspired and impressed by such things, but surely they wouldn't have been silly enough to let this strange and rather large horse into their city without checking it first. Surely there was a simpler, less time-consuming and expensive way for the Greeks to get inside Troy. A battering ram, perhaps? How about just outnumbering the guards?

Just because something is dumb, of course, doesn't mean it's not a good story. I've read enough Dan Brown novels to know that. (Well, I've only read *one*, but that was all I needed.) But here's the silliest thing: for all its dumbness, people think that the Trojan War *really happened*.

Thanks to archaeologists like Heinrich Schliemann, there is evidence that Troy really did exist. The details on the war, however, are based on one bit of "evidence": the *Iliad*. As this is regarded as a great literary work, rather than a work of history, it is strange that we talk of the Trojan War as if it were a real event. We can only wonder if scholars in the far future will talk of Scarlett O'Hara, Batman, and Harry Potter as if they were real people (or at least "based on real people"), the way scholars talk of Helen, Paris, and Achilles as if they must have been real.

It's a nice idea, but if they were based on real people, they must have changed considerably by the time the story was written down. It would be great to think that there was someone as lovely as Helen (even *The Guinness Book of Records* previously had her listed as the most beautiful woman in history), but Homer also said that she was "hatched from a swan's egg." As for Achilles, the whole invincibility thing suggests that he was no more real than Heracles or Apollo (and yes, they were probably fictitious). This is from Homer, the guy who gave us the *Odyssey* (if indeed that was the same writer), with its tales of one-eyed giants and sorceresses turning men into pigs. The man (if indeed he was a man) was no historian.

Nothing is known about Homer. It is thought that he was blind, but considering the vivid visual descriptions in his work, that might not be true. There is even the suggestion that the *Iliad* and the *Odyssey* were the work of a committee, but that seems unlikely. Committees don't usually come up with something this good.

However, if he lived, it was a good four centuries after the alleged events of the Trojan War. It is unknown when his works were put into writing, but they began as an oral composition, probably tweaked with each retelling to make them more interesting. (As there were some twenty-eight thousand verses, it must have gone through a few changes.) No wonder that, by the time it was finally transcribed, it was a perfect tale (except for the bit about the horse).

In ancient Rome, however, historians like Thucydides insisted that the whole thing was true, and that Homer was retelling history. Those ancients believed everything! Presumably they didn't have a word for "fiction writer."

Schliemann led six major archaeological campaigns, from 1870 onward, that seemed to uncover the lost city of Troy in what is now Turkey. This was all very exciting, except that the city he excavated was a lot smaller than the one that Homer imagined. Still, he found the "Treasure of Priam," which included an ancient headdress that he called the "Jewels of Helen." He could call them what he liked, but there was nothing to suggest that they really belonged to Troy's King Priam or the lovely Helen.

There is one piece of evidence in favor of the Trojan War. Based on the history of the ancient world, it is likely that Greece and Troy did indeed go to war over something at least once. Homer was not the first poet to write about the war, and he relied heavily on the work of earlier poets. However, we can't assume that he left the basic facts untouched.

You probably want the story of the Trojan War to be true—and so do I. So have many people over the millennia, which may help to explain why so many people take it seriously. Sadly, there's no evidence, and what's more, when you think about it, it's probably the single dumbest battle plan in military history.

THE TOP 10 MOST
OVERRATED THINGS

◆ ◆ ◆

Most of this book has been about things that are overrated for one or two reasons. The following things, however, are so overrated that they belong in a Hall of Fame (and being overrated, that's probably where they are). They deserve to be exposed.

10. Left and Right Politics

Anyone would think that politics is simple. Everybody is either "right-wing" (worried about the economy, defense, expansion, and free enterprise) or "left-wing" (worried more about unity, social justice, welfare, and the environment). Easy, right?

Okay then, smarty-pants, answer this one: Was Thomas

Jefferson, possibly the greatest statesman ever to be president (and almost certainly the most brilliant mind), a right-winger or a left-winger?

Back in Jefferson's day, politics wasn't divided into "left" and "right." But let's look at the details: he supported a meritocracy and promoted free enterprise and small government. Obviously keen on expansion, he made the Louisiana Purchase from Napoleon, doubling the land area of the United States. Ever the visionary, he was obviously a right-winger before the term was ever coined.

But wait! He was also a strong supporter of the arts. He was a pacifist, avoiding the Napoleonic wars in Europe. He even placed an embargo on American foreign trade to force the European powers to respect American maritime rights. Sounds like a leftie to me.

Commentators from both the Left and the Right have claimed Jefferson, or at least used his actions and quotes, to support their causes, so who's, er, right? "It's all been separated for entertainment value," says Eric S. Petersen, a New York–based Thomas Jefferson scholar. "They need to make it all black-and-white, right and wrong. It's very superficial." Petersen reckons that Jefferson would have scoffed at such division—and he did. "We are all Republicans; we are all Federalists," Jefferson proclaimed in his inaugural speech (when the major parties were the Federalists and his own party, the Republican Democrats; yes, that's what they were called).

Like so much else, politics has been oversimplified. Politicians are labeled "left" and "right," or "liberal" and "conservative." Over the past few decades, things have been simplified so much that Republicans have become "right-wing" and Democrats are "left-wing." So right-wingers decided that one of the great left-wing villains was President Bill Clinton, even though his focus on the economy (including his campaign slogan "It's the economy, stupid!") sounds strangely right-wing. His vice president, Al Gore, is labeled left-wing for his environmental work, but that may surprise people from years gone by, because conservation used to be a conservative issue (which, if you think about it, makes more sense). Christianity, so keenly adopted by right-wingers, was once a left-wing thing—which also makes sense, because Jesus was possibly less inspired by free enterprise and economics than by welfare.

Does this all make sense to you? As you can see, we can't even oversimplify things properly!

"There's this TV program, *Crossfire*," said journalist and author Joe Klein in a 2002 interview, "which begins, 'From the Left, James Carville; from the Right, Robert Novak.' I come from Queens, and what I've tried to do is a balanced accounting."

Still, these "Left" and "Right" labels are useful for a few things:

Dramatic Tension

It's good guys versus bad guys—and best of all, even the audience argues about who the good guys are! The media would love us to pick sides. "The polarization creates conflict, and conflict makes for prodigious amounts of press," wrote Cal Thomas and Bob Beckel in their book *Common Ground: How to Stop the Partisan War That Is Destroying America*. "Could Ann Coulter [conservative commentator and TV personality] sell her factually challenged books or Michael Moore [progressive filmmaker and, er,

TV personality] sell tickets to his selectively edited films
if America was not polarized?"

Making Excuses

"History will treat me fairly," said ex-president Nixon in
1990. "Historians probably won't, because most historians are on the Left." Oh, is that why they were so mean?
Here I thought it was because he and his administration
were corrupt. But no, they just picked on Nixon because
they're a bunch of lefties!

All-Purpose Labeling

Using this Left-Right system, everyone can easily be
labeled—friends, writers, television characters, public
figures, and, of course, the media. "At the *New Republic* in
the 1980s, when I was the editor, we used to joke about
changing our name to 'Even the Liberal New Republic,'
because that was how we were referred to whenever we
took a conservative position on something, which was
often," wrote U.S. commentator Michael Kinsley in the
New York Times. "Then came the day when we took a
liberal position on something and we were referred to as
'Even the Conservative New Republic.'"

Denouncing Your Enemies

Think your opponent is left-wing? Just call him "Stalinist."
Stalin was, of course, famously left-wing. He was also a
tyrannical monster who killed millions of people. Conclusion: left-wingers are tyrannical monsters.

  Using this logic, left-wingers could compare their right-
wing enemies to Hitler—except that, according to Godwin's law, they'd "lose." This theory, devised by attorney

Mike Godwin, suggests that someone "loses" an argument once they do something as over-the-top as comparing their opponent to Hitler or the Nazis. (Comparing people to Stalin because they care for the environment or oppose a war, however, is presumably okay.)

Happily, proud left-wingers rarely reference Hitler. Instead, they have a tradition of calling people "fascist," which is presumably more helpful.

Avoiding Perfectly Good Ideas

Early in the Cold War, a lot of social welfare policy became *damnatio memoriae** in American political discussion. "It got pegged as socialistic and was coded as akin to Soviet communism and therefore opposed to freedom," said historian Eric Foner in 2008. "We don't have public health care in the U.S. because of the phrase 'socialized medicine.'"

Blaming the Media

American right-wingers often accuse the media of "liberal bias" or "left-wing bias." American journalist Bernard Goldberg wrote in his 2001 bestseller, *Bias: A CBS Insider Exposes How the Media Distort the News*, that the media repeatedly identified politicians and writers as "conservative" without labeling their "liberal" counterparts. Like other critics who make such claims, he didn't back it up with facts.

A few months later, Geoffrey Nunberg, a commentator on the National Public Radio show *Fresh Air*, did some

---

* A Latin phrase, meaning "removed from the remembrance." See? This book really is a scholarly work!

research, looking up ten well-known politicians in thirty major U.S. newspapers. He came back with a hundred thousand references. The result: the imbalance in labeling was on the other side. Liberals had a 30 percent greater chance of being labeled than conservatives, even at "liberal" newspapers like the *New York Times*.

Whatever "liberal" is supposed to mean.

9. The Sixties

For over a century we have been reinventing past decades to make them more appealing. People have looked back longingly on the "gay nineties" (that was the 1890s, when "gay" meant something else), the "roaring twenties," even the "sizzling seventies." But no decade has been hyped as much as the 1960s. As remembered by baby boomers, looking back fondly on their youth, this was the decade when *everything* happened.

"If you remember the sixties, you weren't there," quipped Robin Williams. Naturally, he was talking about the drugs, but perhaps, accidentally, he had a good point. Those of us born after the sixties know all about the decade: a perennially cool time when everyone was protesting for civil rights and against the Vietnam War, attending rock festivals and Beatles concerts, living a sexual revolution. Of course, *we weren't actually there*.

Sure, the sixties was a decade of sociocultural change—but so is every other decade. In truth, peace lovers and Vietnam protesters were a vocal minority in the sixties. More people were still voting for conservative politicians, watching *The Sound of Music*, and making sure that women stayed in the home where they belonged.

You already know about the hip, cool, all-time radical, revolutionary, world-changing, way-out stuff that happened in the sixties. Now here's an alternative look at the decade . . .

1960. The contraceptive pill was placed on the market. This shouldn't have been quite as world-changing as it was, but men jumped for joy that a birth-control method had been invented that put all the responsibility on women (unlike all those devices, like condoms, that had been around for hundreds of years). The Pill led to a "sexual revolution," which presumably means that everyone was celibate before this.

Meanwhile, John F. Kennedy, a young and progressive leader, was elected president. Did that prove that the United States was looking to the future? Not really. He defeated the ultraconservative Richard Nixon so narrowly that some people were convinced that he'd lost.

More important, Australian tennis player Neale Fraser won Wimbledon.

1961. With a dashing new president, the ominous, Cold War world of the fifties was transformed completely with . . . the Bay of Pigs invasion, the space race, the break in diplomatic relations with Cuba, the entry of U.S. troops into Vietnam, and the construction of the Berlin Wall. Terrific. Now we had the ominous, Cold War world of the *sixties!*

But that was okay, because many commentators believe that the sixties hadn't actually begun yet, even though the name of the year started with "196." According to such people, the sixties didn't begin until around 1966 (and finished in 1973 or thereabouts). Of course, this would suggest that "sixties" is really the wrong name for the whole thing.

Whether or not this was the sixties, it's worth noting that Rod Laver (Australia) won Wimbledon.

1962. Forget President Kennedy; the immensely popular Republican Senator Barry Goldwater was the *real* political hero of young Americans this year, mostly because he hated Communists as much as they did. "Conservatism is young, virulent, and alive: the wave of the future," he said, accurately enough. So much for the radical sixties.

But change was on the horizon. Nelson Mandela led the antiapartheid movement in South Africa; Martin Luther King campaigned against racism in the United States; and comedian Lenny Bruce appeared at Carnegie Hall, with his searing attacks on racism and injustice. Naturally, all of them were thrown in jail. That's what happened to revolutionaries back then. (Then again, Bruce was arrested for using bad language and King spent a few weeks in the slammer for the heinous crime of holding a prayer meeting. They definitely had good reason to be punished.)

Rod Laver won Wimbledon again. He was *not* thrown in jail.

1963. Bob Dylan became the Voice of the Generation, a title that he never took seriously. Indeed, he claimed that he wasn't always sure what he was singing about, even though he wrote his own songs. Listen to the lyrics of his most significant songs, including "Blowing in the Wind" and "Like a Rolling Stone," and you might be able to understand his confusion.

The world was shocked when President Kennedy was assassinated at forty-six—which is remarkably old for someone known for his youth and vigor (at least in the decade that gave us the advice to "Never trust anyone over thirty").

Margaret Court won Wimbledon. Naturally, she was Australian.

1964. The Beatles came to America—and with them came Beatlemania, as their fans reacted with a hysteria never before seen among pop stars (unless you count Sinatra in the forties, Elvis in the fifties, et al) and never to be seen again (unless you count, ooh, practically everyone since then). At their concerts, the fans were screaming so loudly that they couldn't possibly hear the band play. That might explain why "She Loves You" was so popular.

To reflect the cool, happening music scene, the top box-office movies were the musicals *Mary Poppins* and *My Fair Lady*, and *Billboard*'s top-selling album was the original cast album from *Hello, Dolly!* In these exciting times, President Johnson won the presidential election in a landslide, partly by accusing his opponent, Barry Goldwater, of being "trigger-happy" in Vietnam. As Johnson had been escalating the conflict himself (and would go on to make things even worse), the idea that he was the progressive, "peace" candidate might seem laughable, except that the voters didn't have much choice.

Goldwater, however, still had a following, because he stood for freedom. He opposed the Civil Rights Act, for example, because it infringed the freedom of the states and private-property owners to do whatever they damn well wanted.

Another Australian won Wimbledon. The entire world applauded (or should have done so).

1965. One of the most popular TV shows was *The Man from U.N.C.L.E.*, which inspired a worldwide fashion trend for—wait for it—*polo-necked Skivvies*! Sorry, but the decade wasn't all miniskirts and psychedelic vests. In fact, few people were wearing either in 1965. Race-goers were shocked when British model Jean Shrimpton wore a miniskirt to the opening day of the Melbourne Cup horse race in Australia, revealing an extra four inches of flesh. People obviously lived rather sheltered lives in those days.

Meanwhile, the Vietnam conflict escalated at an alarming rate, as President Johnson sent in the marines to turn a bad situation even worse. A few people protested, but it wasn't as shocking as Jean Shrimpton's miniskirt.

Timothy Leary was preaching LSD as a spiritual experience, telling his followers to "turn on, tune in, drop out." Proof that the radical youth of the sixties were so dedicated to improving the world that they spent most of their time trying to escape it.

The most exciting event of the year: *two* Aussie singles players won Wimbledon, proving beyond doubt that Australia was easily the greatest nation on Earth.

1966. A cultural revolution shaped the lives of millions. Now this was the *real* sixties! No, we're not talking about anything cool or hip that was going on in London or San Francisco, but *the* Cultural Revolution, as Chairman Mao dealt with the liberal forces who threatened to destroy his ideal Communist state with their "bourgeois reactionary thinking." Millions of young people's lives would be changed forever . . . by death.

Things were more progressive in the United States, where—as if foretelling the exciting changes that were destined to occur in youth culture—LSD was made illegal. Sadly, this didn't stop Timothy Leary from his usual ravings.

The Vietnam War, meanwhile, was extremely popular. Of course, it inspired many of the most popular songs. In

1966, *Billboard*'s top-selling single was . . . "The Ballad of the Green Berets" by SSgt. Barry Sadler, a salute to the heroes of war. I don't believe that Joan Baez ever covered this song.

Time magazine's "Man of the Year" (it wasn't "Person of the Year" back then) was the "25-and-under" generation, as the magazine boldly predicted seven milestones that the kids would achieve, such as landing on the moon (check), curing the common cold (er, not yet), ensuring world peace, and . . . well, one out of seven will have to do.

Meanwhile, at Wimbledon . . . nothing important happened.

1967. To many, this is known as rock music's greatest year, thanks to all the "classic" albums. The top-selling album of the year? *Sgt. Pepper's Lonely Hearts Club Band*? Something by Dylan? Actually, the two highest sellers were *both* by the Monkees, a band manufactured for a TV show (followed by the soundtracks to *Dr. Zhivago* and *The Sound of Music*). It was also the year that Love, Pink Floyd, and the Velvet Underground released great rock albums, but despite what you might think, almost no one bought them. True, a few hip, groovy people forked out the money, but *most* people were not actually groovy enough to listen to "happening" sixties music back in the sixties.

Meanwhile, Latin American freedom fighter Che Guevara died, little knowing that millions of people would one day wear his face on their T-shirts in a desperate attempt to look cool and revolutionary, without actually knowing what he did.

After the terrible drought of 1966, another Aussie won Wimbledon.

1968. Much has been written about this year. Author Mark Kurlansky, in his book about 1968, called it "the year that rocked the world." *Time* magazine called it an *annus mirabilis* (which is Latin, so it must have been important). Old-timers, comparing it to the far more devastating years of World War II, must have been rolling their eyes.

Still, 1968 had more than its share of violent events. Martin Luther King and Robert Kennedy were both assassinated. Did this make them martyrs, inspiring their supporters to continue their work? Sadly, it didn't seem to do a great deal. Kennedy had been running for president, but the election was instead won by Richard Nixon, with a conservative, pro-Vietnam agenda. Meanwhile, Broadway presented the musical of the sixties, *Hair*, in which a group of youngsters announced the greatest statement of the generation: their intention to grow really long hair. Awriiiight! Try to stop *that*, Nixon!

Rod Laver, possibly the greatest sportsman in history, won Wimbledon again.

1969. Much fuss was made when three astronauts visited the moon. It was a sign of our space-faring future. (We're still waiting . . .) The Vietnam War became worse, making leaders realize that, in the future, world problems would be solved with peaceful solutions. (We're still waiting . . .) Meanwhile, five hundred thousand people attended Woodstock, an important event on the path to world peace. (We're still waiting . . .) In such a vintage year for music, Billboard's top-selling single was . . . "Sugar Sugar," a cutesy song by the Archies, a make-believe cartoon band (based on a wholesome, twenty-nine-year-old comic book). Whoa, hold me down!

Oh, and Rod Laver (still Australian) won Wimbledon again.

◆   ◆   ◆

But were the sixties still worth the hype? After all, they did give us Rachel Carson, Spider-Man, weather satellites, and (in primitive form) the Internet. Still, none of those won as much attention at the time as *Sgt. Pepper* or Woodstock. The "highlights" of the sixties, it would seem, were the times that people thought they were changing the world, but probably weren't.

As the next year was called 1970, you could argue that the sixties finished in 1969. In the seventies, nothing would be nearly as good . . .

Good in the Sixties, *Better* in the Seventies

David Bowie

Doctor Who

The environmental movement

Heart transplants

Hot-pants fashion statements

Jack Nicholson

Mark Spitz

Monty Python

Simon and Garfunkel

The women's movement

8. Statistics

A famous quote, usually attributed to Mark Twain (who attributed it to Disraeli), says that statistics are one of three types of lies, along with "lies" and "damned lies" (which are at least honest about being lies). Still, everyone seems to trust statistics. The latest book I was perusing is littered with statistics all the way through—and as that was *this* book, I knew that even cynical writers tend to put too much trust in statistics.

The truth is, many statistics are unreliable: biased, selective, misleading, misused, misinterpreted, misunderstood, or just plain silly. You've probably heard the line that, statistically, it's safer to travel by airline than by car. That might seem to make sense, because twenty times more people die in car accidents than in airline crashes.

The thing is, nobody is really sure how many journeys are made by car, but you can be sure it's zillions more than the number of plane trips. (No, "zillions" is not a statistical figure.) I hate to scare you away from flying (which is still much safer than, say, alligator wrestling), but you have considerably more chance of surviving a car journey than surviving a flight.

In most cases, of course, statistics are only based on a selection, not the whole, and sometimes, the selection is slightly distorted. Have you ever heard the figure (often quoted by gay rights campaigners) that one in ten men are gay? You may have, thanks to Alfred Kinsey's landmark 1953 report *Sexual Behavior in the Human Male* (also called the "Kinsey Report"). Wanting to explore a broad range of sexual experiences, Kinsey interviewed a good number of active homosexuals and prison inmates. The report noted that "10 percent of the males are more or less exclusively homosexual . . . for at least three years." Great, but he was talking about people *in the survey*.

The true figure? We can't really tell. Kinsey did his research in 1950s America, when not every gay male was likely to admit to his sexuality. Even in these supposedly more open-minded times, surveys can't be trusted to tell us such things.

Other statistics simply don't make sense, but are still published. Sociologist Joel Best once noted a statistic published in 1995: "Every year since 1950, the number of American children gunned down has doubled." Assuming that only one child was gunned down in 1950, this would have been up to one billion (more than four times the U.S. population) by 1980, and 35 *trillion* by 1995. That would be simply terrible.

Best contacted the author of this statistic, who said that it came from a reputable organization, the Children's Defense Fund. Sure enough, the CDF's 1994 yearbook claimed: "The number of American children killed each year by guns has doubled since 1950." Oh, now that's *different*. Still dramatic, perhaps . . . until some spoilsport (like me) tells you that the U.S. population grew by 73 percent. You can expect everything else, including shootings, to grow as well.

Other stats, of course, are perfectly legit. You just have to know their source, their bias, and whether they make any sense. This might not be as easy as it sounds, especially if the source has a valid-sounding name like the Council on Public Opinion (which was exposed in 1938 as a group of America's top propagandists).

Here are some other great statistics:

♦ In the 1970s, a motoring magazine reported that the average life for a Corvette in a New York City parking lot—before it was stolen—was one hour. This was terrible news for Corvette owners, afraid to park in NYC. Happily, the only people surveyed for this statistic were the owners of stolen Corvettes. Most parked Corvettes were *not* stolen . . . but if they were, it was usually sooner rather than later, which was surely no great scoop.

♦ Activists like to quote statistics, especially when it highlights the seriousness of their issue. Mitch Snyder, a leading advocate for the homeless, said in the early 1980s that there were 2 to 3 million homeless people in America. When Ted Koppel quizzed him about this on *Nightline*, Snyder explained: "Everyone demanded it. Everybody said, 'We want a number.' . . . We got on the phone, we made a lot of calls, we talked to a lot of people, and we said, 'Okay, here are some numbers.' They have no meaning, no value."

♦ Stalking was a crime du jour of the 1990s, with *U.S. News & World Report* saying that "researchers suggest that up to 200,000 people exhibit a stalker's traits." Other media "expanded" on this. "There are an estimated 200,000 stalkers in the United States—and those are only the ones that we have track of," said Sally Jessy Raphael, that doyenne of serious tele-journalism. "Some 200,000 people in the U.S. pursue the famous," said an article in *Cosmopolitan*. "No one knows how many people stalk the rest of us, but that figure is probably higher." It got scarier every time . . .

◆ How many Americans have been abducted by UFOs? Excellent question, and one that was answered in a national survey in 1993. But rather than ask an obvious question like "Have you ever been abducted by aliens?"—the researchers decided that people would be unwilling to talk about it (or, aliens being what they are, they might have had their memories wiped). Instead, they framed their questions around five symptoms that abductees often claimed to suffer (like "Have you ever woken up paralyzed with a sense of a strange person or presence of something else in the room?"). If anyone said yes to four or more symptoms, they were probably abducted. As it happened, 2 percent fell into this group, so according to the survey, 2 percent had been abducted.

◆ In their constant search for hype, Hollywood studios like to promote certain box-office stats. We've already exposed *Titanic*, the so-called biggest box-office film of all time. Now, "the most *profitable* movie of all time" is *Paranormal Activity*, a film made by novice filmmakers, famous for its ultralow budget. It cost around $15,000, which would barely have paid for Kate Winslet's eye shadow in *Titanic*. Its worldwide earnings, however, are $107.9 million at time of writing. So far, it's made back its money 7,193 times over. It's safe to say that other movies haven't done that. If the mega-budget *Titanic* had made 7,193 times its cost, it would have made more than $1.4 *trillion* (which is around 780 times the world record, and enough to run several nations). So even though *Titanic* and about three hundred other movies made more money, *Paranormal Activity* is the most *profitable*. Aren't percentages cool? (Another phrase that gets published a lot is "fastest-growing." If you sold one piece of caramel fudge at a market stall and sold two pieces the next week, doubling your previous week's profits, your little fudge-making enterprise would be growing faster than Wal-Mart!)

+ One of my favorite stats was explained on the BBC television series *QI*. Statistically, we have twice as much chance of being killed by an asteroid as by a bolt of lightning. Sure, nobody has been killed by an asteroid *yet*, but asteroids hit the Earth every millon years, and the next one's running late. A "dangerous" asteroid is 1.2 miles in diameter, which could strike with the equivalent of a million megatons of TNT, wiping out a billion people. Hence, the chance of death by asteroid is one in 6 million. Many people have been struck by lightning, but our chances of dying this way are only one in 10 million. Lucky us.

+ According to a *Time* magazine poll in 2002, 37 percent of the Americans who considered themselves vegetarian had eaten red meat in the previous twenty-four hours; 60 percent had eaten some kind of meat or seafood. Perhaps they didn't understand the term. (A vegetarian is someone who doesn't eat meat, not even poultry or fish. I thought I'd mention it, just in case.)

• It's about time someone answered the question "Do voters choose candidates for their looks?" Rather than surveying people (because most people would vehemently deny such a thing), a pair of Australian academics embarked on a major study in 2006, looking at the major-party candidates in the 2004 Australian election to see if the hunks and hotties were getting the votes. And who decided who was a "hunk" or a "hottie"? *Five people.* Nothing against the "most beautiful" candidate—blond, thirty-three-year-old science graduate Nicole Campbell (who didn't win, for the record)—but a major academic survey should be based on more than five people looking at photos and saying "She's not bad" or "Man, what a babe!" or whatever scientific commentary they used. What did the survey reveal? The professors weren't sure (except that, according to five people, Nicole was a looker).

• What nation has the world's highest crime rate? Statistically, it's the Vatican, which might surprise you because it's supposed to have the holiest population, familiar with the teachings of Christ. In case you're afraid of getting mugged by a nun, however, the Vatican's high crime rate is due to its small population (fewer than one thousand) and the crowds of tourists, which make it a popular spot for pickpockets. Hence, it has 1.5 crimes per citizen. Some stats are just plain misleading.

7. High IQs

Given the choice, most of us would like a high intelligence—and it's perfectly normal, even healthy, to admit that. Like the Scarecrow in *The Wizard of Oz*, wistfully singing "If I only had a brain," we long to have extra brainpower. If we said we'd like to be wealthier or more beautiful, it would seem shallow. But if we were really smart, we'd probably have more money, and we wouldn't even need to be beautiful.

The most common way intelligence is measured is by IQ (intelligence quotient). Those with high IQs possess fast and accurate reasoning and analytical skills. They are probably good at math puzzles. It doesn't necessarily mean that they can discuss the works of Proust in a profound and entertaining way, win a game of Trivial Pursuit, or even hold a knife and fork properly. In fact, here's the real shocker: *they might not even be highly intelligent.*

There's no universal consensus about what intelligence actually is. Some believe it's the ability to adapt to a foreign environment; others say that it's the ability to think abstractly; and there are many more qualities that are often described as "intelligent." Someone's IQ—or their score on an IQ test, at least—can be affected strongly by environment or other biases in the test.

Technically, a "genius" is someone whose IQ is in the top 2 percent of the population, scoring 132 or higher on the Stanford-Binet test (or the equivalent on another standardized exam). And what would you get for being so clever? You would be eligible for Mensa, the association for the superintelligent. (*Mensa* is the Latin word for "table." They wanted to use the Latin word for "mind," but that's *mens*, which apparently sounds too much like a dirty magazine. Perhaps you need to be really smart to understand that.) When it started in Britain in 1946, the founders of Mensa had a vision to forward a list of Britain's six hundred brightest people to the government, which could then have easy access to the best minds in times of crisis. No government has ever used this advice (as you could have probably guessed), but Mensa now claims one hundred thousand members worldwide.

So if they don't get to serve their country, why do they join? If they're so smart, why did they pay $40 simply to take the test? Is it the prestige of showing that they are from the high-IQ elite, in the footsteps of Einstein, da Vinci, Copernicus, and other geniuses?

If this is why they want to join, they might as well forget about it. As far as we know, Einstein, whose name is synonymous with all things ingenious, never had an IQ test, but experts believe that his great discoveries were due not so much to his IQ, but to his great level of "transcendental thinking." In other words, he had a high degree of creativity and imagination. Someone with an IQ of 200, for all their official genius, might not have the creative ability to devise the Theory of Relativity. Einstein spent time on his equations, raising his thinking to superhigh levels.

Obviously, da Vinci and Copernicus never had IQ tests, but in 1926, psychologist Catherine Morris Cox published a study estimating the IQs of "eminent men and women" of the past, based largely on the intelligence shown by these people in their childhood (which might not be the best way to do it, but I don't know of any better way). In this study, da Vinci scored 135—a Mensa qualifier, as you'd expect (though still not as bright as Voltaire, Galileo, and Napoleon).

Copernicus, however, scored a decidedly average 105— which was obviously enough to make him an astronomer, a mathematician, a physician, a classical scholar, a translator, a cleric, a statesman, a military leader, a diplomat, and an economist. Presumably, like Einstein, his genius was in his creative ability.

According to its website, Mensa seeks to "identify and foster human intelligence for the benefit of humanity, to encourage research in the nature, characteristics and uses of intelligence, and to promote stimulating intellectual and social opportunities for its members." The government might not want them, but the New York chapter of Mensa has been used in marketing, devising ingenious ideas for companies ranging from dog food companies to Roto-Rooter.

Most of all, however, it's a social forum. In 2001, the *New York Times* eavesdropped on a Mensa gathering, in which one member, Ron Ruemmler, made a quip about "slumming at Yale University." The group found this very amusing. "You see, everyone knew what I was getting at without me having to spell it out," said Mr. Ruemmler. For the record, he was making a snide comment about Yale graduate George W. Bush. "Somewhere else . . . I might have to explain everything, which would slow it all down. With Mensa, you know most everyone would get the reference."

Did you get it? If you did—and even if you didn't— such a scene might help to explain the attraction of Mensa. "We actually get your jokes," they announced in a

2007 magazine advertisement. These Mensans (as they are called, perhaps in a deliberate attempt to sound like aliens) can mingle with others like themselves. Many of them have admitted that, outside the group, they feel like outcasts. It's like an obsessive stamp collector meeting others with an encyclopedic knowledge of stamps, or comic book fans going to a convention and arguing passionately about who would win a fight between Captain Marvel and the Hulk.

Naturally, a high IQ is cool, but it hardly deserves the reverence that is usually attached to it. Canadian scientist David Suzuki (who is undoubtedly very smart, but not necessarily a Mensa candidate) once wrote that: "In a city the size of Montreal, there may be 100,000 or more people who would score higher than 120. But so what? What does an IQ score tell us about the enormous human variability that resides in all the people who share that number? They will have just as many stupid, mean, avaricious, generous, caring individuals as any other group." (Notice the word "stupid." Even geniuses can have that problem.)

Perhaps, rather than worship our minds and covet higher intelligence like the Scarecrow (who was, by his own admission, brainless), we should instead follow the advice of the Tin Woodsman, who longed for a heart— and you assume he didn't mean the cardiac muscle, but the spiritual heart, complete with its conscience, its kindness, and its altruism. Now *there's* something you can use to serve your country!

6. The Olympic Spirit

The story is told every four years. Baron Pierre de Coubertin, a young French aristocrat, started the modern Olympic Games to foster sporting excellence and, even more important, world peace and harmony—the principles, he believed, upon which the ancient Olympics had been founded.

It was great that he had this inspiration, but he had his history all wrong. The origins of the Olympics are uncertain, but the original purpose was almost certainly to keep men fit for battle, hence events like javelin throwing and race-in-armor (in which runners would run wearing helmets and leg armor, carrying their shields). Not so peaceful, really.

Even if it wasn't founded for military reasons, the other theories aren't exactly for pacifists. One celebrated legend is that Pelops wanted to marry Hippodamia, daughter of King Oenomaus of Elis. Oenomaus had a novel way to test whether his daughter's suitors were worthy: he challenged them to a chariot race. If they lost (which invariably happened), they were killed. Pelops, however, possessed one of the great Olympic talents: corruption. He bribed Oenomaus's charioteer to sabotage his chariot, so that a wheel spun off during the race and Oenomaus was killed. Pelops then married Hippodamia and began the Olympics. So it seems that cheating has been part of the Olympics since day one—and so, for the record, has murder.

You might assume that the games themselves were far nicer. Perhaps the opening ceremonies were graceful affairs, like the classical dance in the 2004 Athens opening ceremony. Or maybe not. As the early games opened, priests and officials made speeches, dedicating them to Zeus, king of the gods. They would then order some slaves to drive oxen to the Great Altar, slaughtering them one by one. (The oxen, not the slaves.) They would continue this slaughter for the rest of the night, as the crowd—realizing that there was only so much entertainment value in watching this—dispersed. So many cattle were slaughtered over the years that the great altar of Zeus, which oversaw each of the Greek games, was not built of stone, but of burned animal carcasses, congealed with blood and fat.

Naturally, things improved once the sports started. Not much, though. Two thousand years later, Baron de Coubertin would stress that "the important thing in the Olympic Games is not winning but taking part." The Olympians of the time, however, were literally willing to kill to win, and in many sports, the crowd was willing to see just that. As this was a religious event (like most other aspects of ancient Greek society), a champion was regarded as touched by divinity, raised above the status of mortals. Exactly how this differs from the modern Olympics, I'm not sure.

They would even resort to performance-enhancing substances. For wrestlers and boxers, fly agaric mushrooms were the anabolic steroids of the era. They were poisonous, but mind-bending enough to give them the madness they required to push themselves to the limit. Meanwhile, chariot racers doped their horses with hydromel (which was only a mixture of honey and water, but it sure *sounds* illegal).

As you may be aware, part of the ancient Olympic ideal (and de Coubertin's own vision) was that women were banned. Well, almost. Every Olympics, a mini-Olympic competition was held for unmarried women known as the Heraia (dedicated to Hera, queen of the gods). The historian Pausanias wrote that married women found at the Olympics "on the days when they were forbidden to enter" were duly prosecuted, that is, thrown off a cliff. It is thought that the athletes started performing naked, and the crowd was also ordered to disrobe, just in case any of them were women in disguise. That was the excuse, at least.

The baron was also inspired by the Olympic truce, in which all wars would stop so that the nations could engage in the friendly spirit of competition. Once again, he didn't get it exactly right. True, the Greek states held the three-month Olympic Truce during every festival, in which they were forbidden to go to war, carry on disputes in law courts, or execute criminals. (Anyone who broke the truce was heavily fined.) But this was not a sign of amity as much as a practical way of ensuring that the competitors and spectators could make it to the games without getting lynched. Since everyone had the same gods, they would drop everything—even their weapons— for this religious event.

Whatever the reason, it was a remarkable thing (when it worked). Sometimes, the urge to beat each other senseless overcame the urge to appease the gods. Just as the modern Olympics were canceled during the two world wars, the ancient Olympics were also often canceled due to war, which in both cases defeated the whole purpose. Spartans were banned from the games during the Peloponnesian Wars simply because Athens and Elis were on the other side. In 424 BC, armed security forces surrounded the stadium in case of Spartan attack.

The history of the ancient Olympics is not exactly peaceful. In the second century BC, the games moved to Rome after the Romans invaded Greece, plundering the temples. The games were finally banned by Emperor Theodosius in AD 393 because they had devolved into a shady carnival, full of cheating, bribery, gambling, and (gasp) *professionalism*.

Of course, you could use the same excuses if you wanted to cancel the modern Olympics. But for all the sorry moments in their history, the current Games are a generally inspired—and inspiring—event. The best thing about the ancient Olympics was not the reality, but what they accidentally stood for, all those years later. Thank goodness Baron de Coubertin got it so wrong.

◇◇◇

Great Ancient Olympic Events

BOXING
Instead of boxing gloves, boxers wore strips of leather around their hands, which didn't exactly soften the blow. One fighter is said to have shoved his fingers into his opponent's stomach so hard that he pulled out his guts. A fight ended when one fighter surrendered . . . or died. Take your pick.

WRESTLING
Wrestlers could do anything, apart from biting and digging their fingers into soft parts of the body like the eyes and the groin. After hair-pulling became a popular move, wrestlers started the long tradition of shaving their heads.

PANKRATION

One of the most popular events, pankration was a blend of boxing and wrestling, with some judo thrown in. Compared to pankration, those other sports were for wimps. This was basically a one-on-one brawl, in which the competing wrestlers/boxers/hooligans were allowed to do anything, save biting and eye-gouging, until their opponents either died or begged for mercy. Sostratos, one of the most celebrated champions, was famous for wrenching his opponents' ankles out of their sockets.

◇◇

5. "Proper English"

From our school days on, the rules of grammar are fastidiously hammered into our heads. But are they much use to anyone (apart from those clever people who like to demonstrate their superiority by correcting other people's grammatical slips)?

Okay, the English language is one of the world's most widespread forms of communication, and if we misunderstand one another, it can be disastrous. That's why we should know the basics of grammar, as well as spelling and punctuation. It gets a bit trivial, however, when someone tells you off for saying "which" when you should have said "that."

After all, many great authors have messed around with grammar—from the present-tense street lingo of Damon Runyon and the New Zealand Maori slang of Alan Duff (complete with—gasp!—*misspellings*) to the working-class Scottish vernacular of Irvine Welsh or Alan Spence—and based on their success, it was all perfectly readable, even splendid. Then there was a gentleman named Shakespeare. When I first read some of Shakespeare's plays (and in my defense, I was rather young), I was so well honed on proper grammar that I was alarmed with his inaccuracies, from starting sentences with the word "And" to using the wrong tense. Didn't he know the basics of writing?

And therein lies the problem with "proper English." The language is constantly changing and developing. Just as new words are frequently being added to the dictionary, new grammatical rules also apply. Shakespeare might be the greatest writer in the history of the language, but the English language he used four hundred years ago was noticeably different to ours. It was also very different from Middle English, the language that Geoffrey Chaucer used to write *The Canterbury Tales* two hundred years before Shakespeare's time. Though it is often mistakenly called "Old English," *real* Old English was spoken by the Saxons before the Norman Conquest of 1066—and is *completely* different. To us, learning Old English would be like learning French or Swahili.

But of all the rules of grammar people will scold you for breaking, which are the most overrated ones? Three types come to mind:

Rules That Make Sense in Other Languages, but Are Pointless in English

The split infinitive is a good example, used in such passages as "it is intended to better prepare us for the future" and *Star Trek*'s line "to boldly go where no one has gone before." Maybe it's because of familiarity, but that sounds slightly better than "to go boldly." Fortunately, it's a stylistic "rule" rather than a grammatical one. It's also a leftover from Latin, a language that almost nobody speaks anymore, in which the infinitive is a single word. Splitting a word, of course, would be ri-freakin'-diculous.

Rules That Some Unknown Person Made Up for Some Unknown Reason

This includes such commandments as "Don't end a sentence with a preposition." As ridiculous as this "rule" is, at least it allowed Winston Churchill to use one of his best one-liners: "This is something up with which I will not put."*

Rules That Everyone Gets Wrong

The only thing worse than having your grammar corrected is having your grammar corrected by someone who's completely wrong. As a writer, I get this occasionally. People are especially proud to outwit someone who should know better. With all due respect, however, they're not always correct. Probably the most commonly abused "rule" of grammar is the one about when to use "I" and "me." Finish a sentence by saying "my husband and me" and someone will be quick to correct you (with maximum smugness). This would be unfair, as you were almost certainly right. The actual rule is: "I" in the subjective case, "me" in the objective case. Or, imagine what you'd say if your husband wasn't involved. The correct sentence

---

* At least, we think it was Churchill. Like Mark Twain or Voltaire, many of the lines attributed to him were actually someone else's.

would be "Jack went fishing with my husband and me." If you must say "my husband and I," say "My husband and I went fishing with Jack." If anyone insists otherwise, show them this page of the book. (It has a respectable publisher.)

4. Skepticism

Now let's talk about skeptical people, and how terribly clever they are. They don't believe *anything*. Listening to one of these people, you would assume that nothing really exists. Nobody sounds smarter than a guy who hears, sees, and reads plenty of evidence, and still says, "I don't believe a word of it!"

Ever since the great French philosopher René Descartes doubted his own existence (what sort of loon would doubt *his own existence*?), it has been a sign of intelligence to be skeptical about almost everything.

Skeptics, of course, have done many good things. They have exposed various fortune-tellers, spoon-benders, and other charlatans over the centuries. They have added to social debate and intellectual discussion. However, they don't always get it right.

Rather than go through everything that skeptics deny, which would take several books, let's just use one example:

Conspiracy Theories

Ah yes, conspiracy theories. Like soap operas and numerology, these are something that "clever" people never take seriously. "One thing you've got to remember," said the revered British astronomer Patrick Moore. "When you hear 'conspiracy theory,' that is the hallmark of the crackpot." Those willing to believe that President Kennedy's murder was a conspiracy are denounced as "conspiracy buffs," "conspiracy nuts," "conspiracy junkies," or just plain "paranoids." But according to a 2003 poll, two-thirds of Americans fit into this group.

It's strange that journalists and commentators, so proudly skeptical of most things, are often so willing to accept the official version of events that they won't consider any alternative. The truth is that conspiracies—*proven* conspiracies—have been part of history for millennia. Still, conspiracy skeptics scoff at whatever they hear. When you want to prove your intellectual superiority, you start quoting a philosopher—smart conspiracy skeptics name the Austrian-British philosopher Sir Karl Popper, who scorned the "conspiracy theory of society." Naturally, Sir Karl was an intelligent man who knew what he was talking about. However, he was referring to Lenin, Hitler, and others whose ideas were based (he believed) on paranoid delusions. "I do not wish to imply that conspiracies never happen," he wrote in 1945. "On the contrary, they are typical social phenomena." So the great conspiracy debunker was not a debunker at all! Not so clever now, are you, skeptics?

True, many conspiracy theories seem to be just plain silly. In a 1996 massacre in the Australian tourist town of Port Arthur, thirty-five people were killed by lone gunman Martin Bryant . . . or were they? Five years later, some of Australia's more extreme politicians suggested that Bryant was just a patsy, and the whole thing was a conspiracy by bleeding-heart left-wingers to justify tougher gun laws.

So "bleeding hearts" killed all those people just so the government would ban semiautomatic weapons? (For the record, their fiendish ploy worked.)

Equally hard to believe (though who am I to denounce them?) are various theories about alien abduction, hundred-year-old assassination plots, and American conspiracy theorist Lyndon LaRouche's idea that man-made climate change "is a political campaign spearheaded by Al Gore and piloted by the same people pushing globalization." (As 98 percent of climate scientists are in on this, it would have to be one of the largest conspiracies in history.)

But other theories haven't been quite so outlandish. Abraham Lincoln, of course, was assassinated in 1865. As with Kennedy's death, nearly a century later, rumors soon circulated about a conspiracy. In Lincoln's case, however, it was proven. Three of the conspirators were given life imprisonment; four were executed.

Then there was the 1972 conspiracy theory that President Nixon's reelection campaigners were behind a burglary in the Watergate complex in Washington, DC. It was virtually ignored at the time. The government dismissed it as a "third-rate burglary," so that was that. If you can't trust politicians, who *can* you trust? Case closed.

But then came an annoying pair of long-haired conspiracy buffs, namely Bob Woodward and Carl Bernstein, eager young reporters for the *Washington Post*. As they started to uncover details (with a determination that must have made them look like kooky paranoids), they were scorned. However, they were allowed to keep digging, perhaps because their evidence didn't involve the CIA, flying saucers, the Freemasons, or Elvis (who was officially still alive, of course). It turned out that this was a real conspiracy, and once the truth was known, nobody was laughing at the conspiracy theory.

But what about those really weird, way-out, supernatural theories? Leslie Bohem, creator of the 2003 TV series *Taken* (inspired by stories of alien cover-ups), was open to the possibility of UFO conspiracies in the United States, if only because they made more sense than the alternative. "I love the debunkers," he said. "Fifty people say they saw something, and one guy goes, 'It's a plover bird, but when it turns sideways and the light from a '57 Dodge hits it . . .' It's a more ridiculous explanation than the Venusians!"

Perhaps people want to believe that conspiracy theories are crazy. Obviously, we'd rather believe that we safely know all the facts, that no shady conspiracies are going on under our noses, and that the only bad guys are from faraway lands. Conspiracy theories tend to ruin that for us.

It may be uncomfortable to think that the "evidence" that started the Iraq War was doctored (as proven), or that the Third Reich was part of a larger extraterrestrial plot involving alien abductions, the CIA, and a mysterious group called the Green Dragon Society (okay, that hasn't been proven yet).

Still, conspiracy theories aren't all bad news. Take the one about Jim Morrison conspiring with a few close friends to fake his death, so he could give up rock music and start a new career working as a stockbroker in Paris. Surely you'd like to believe *that* one.

Other Things Skeptics Don't Believe In

Telepathy

Ghosts

Palmistry

Anything That Isn't Scientifically Proven (which presumably means that before Isaac Newton formulated the Laws of Motion, the skeptics were convinced that nothing moved)

The Loch Ness Monster

Religion (because it has led to some terrible things)

God (because He/She/It hasn't been scientifically proven, and because religion has led to some terrible things)

Santa Claus (even though he—or, at least, Saint Nicholas—really existed, as did Casanova, Uncle Sam, Johnny Appleseed, and Lady Godiva; the Easter Bunny is a fake, though)

Most Major Inventions and Discoveries of the Past Five Hundred Years (until they were proven)

Climate Change

3. The Meat-and-Vegetables Diet

Let's face it, we've had some dumb dietary fads over the years, from the unhealthy forty-day juice fast of the seventies to the dangerous extremes of *Dr. Atkins' Diet Revolution* (which has sold millions). But the most overrated diet ever, which has been popular for quite a while, is the ever-popular combination of meat and vegetables. Or, indeed, meat and *anything*.

This probably isn't news to you. Chances are, you've been lectured by an annoying vegetarian friend, who has said things like "How can you possibly eat a poor, defenseless animal, especially a cute one?" or tried to ruin your dining experience with graphic imagery (as poet Alexander Pope did for his readers when he talked of "kitchens covered with blood, and filled with cries of beings expiring in tortures"). There are many, many problems with meat, and when a vegetarian campaigner is fired up, you are in danger of hearing every one of them.

But before you dismiss this chapter as a work of tree-hugging-animal-loving-neo-liberal-hippie extremism, let's ignore most of the reasons why people give up meat—health, moral, and spiritual—and go straight to perhaps the best reason: the environment. Even back in 1990, the Washington research group the Worldwatch Institute reported that we would need "a vegetarian meal in every pot" by 2030 to ensure an "environmentally safe" future.

Agriculture, mainly from livestock, provides nearly a quarter of the world's greenhouse pollution. A team of health experts suggested in 2007 that people in wealthy nations, for their health as well as the ecology, should each have only ninety grams of meat a day, about the same amount as a regular hamburger.

So relax, they only suggested that we should *reduce* our meat consumption, not completely stop eating meat (though if you want to stop, that's perfectly fine). Per capita, meat consumption has more than doubled since 1961. Worldwatch said that if Americans reduced their meat consumption by only 10 percent, 100 million extra people could be fed.

How does this work? Well, you may have heard that countless acres of Amazon rain forest have been cleared for timber over the past few decades. Actually, more of it has been cleared as *grazing land*, including that for millions of pounds of "prime U.S. beef" in South and Central America. Livestock uses—are you sitting down?—*almost a third of the world's ice-free land surface*. Most of this is pasture, but it also includes a third of the world's arable land, dedicated to livestock feed.

Farm animals, as well as needing their space (good-bye, forests), need to eat. Over a lifetime, we're talking a lot of food. It takes thirty-five pounds of grain and soy to produce two pounds of beef, while pork requires thirteen pounds, and chicken needs a relatively economical six pounds. So in the United States, 70 percent of all grain goes to feeding livestock.

American factory farms produce 6 billion animals each year to be eaten. It takes a lot to maintain such a habit, so more than half the water used in the United States goes to livestock production. In California, it takes 24 gallons of water to produce half a kilogram of tomatoes, potatoes, or wheat. To produce the same amount of beef would take 5,212 gallons. "Pass up one hamburger," wrote Worldwatch's Ed Ayres in *Time* magazine, "and you'll save as much water as you save by taking forty showers in a low-flow nozzle." And while we're still talking about livestock, bear in mind that cattle have a gas problem that they probably don't want to talk about, especially since they cause 40 percent of the world's methane emissions.

Of course, some of these emissions are caused by their

waste products. A lot of them, in fact. In America, livestock produces 130 times as much waste as people do. "Just one hog farm in Utah," wrote Ayres, "produces more sewage than the city of Los Angeles."

There are millions of vegetarians in the world, but most of them, of course, are not in developed countries. Surveys over the years have suggested that anywhere between 1 and 7 percent of Americans are vegetarian (though people differ over what "vegetarian" means). Still, we have been told in numerous campaigns that meat is not only healthy but harmless. As you can see, this is not quite true, but meat production is a large and powerful industry. That industry can afford the advertising and public relations to convince everyone, giving us such slogans as "Red meat: we were meant to eat it" and the American Cattlemen's bumper sticker "If animals weren't meant to be eaten, then why are they made out of meat?"

If such logic convinces you, then feel free to continue eating meat. But with all the recent worries about obesity, climate change, ethics, even the cost of living, you can see why experts now suggest that we should eat *less* meat. Sometimes, hippy-trippy animal lovers actually have a point.

<><><><><><><><><><><><><><><><><><><><><><><><><><><><><><><><>

Best of Health

Though people used to give up meat for health reasons, you could argue for days whether or not it's healthier to be vegetarian. Even Michael Moore, the guy America's rednecks are supposed to hate the most, agreed with most of them when he wrote: "Vegetarianism is unhealthy . . . Put down those sprouts and pick up a T-bone!"

So was he right? It depends. It's easy enough to be an unhealthy vegetarian, if you don't have meat-free sources of vitamin B12, iron, and protein. Besides, you can be a vegetarian and still eat appalling amounts of junk. At the same time, meat-related diseases cause more deaths than cigarettes, which suggests that we might be eating too much of it. In Western countries, the most common cause of death is heart disease, and the leading causes of heart attacks are cholesterol and saturated fat.

You don't tend to hear about dogs and cats suffering from heart attacks, but in case you didn't notice it, they are physically very different from us. They have relatively short intestinal tracts—only three times their body length—so meat (which decays quickly) has a speedy passage. Human intestines can be unraveled to eighty-two feet in length. This gives meat enough time to transform into bodily wastes, some of them toxic, increasing the risk of heart disease and several cancers.

Elephants and giraffes, like humans, have intestinal tracts about twelve times their body length. Naturally, they're herbivores.

◇◇

2. The Past

A few years ago, I wrote a book about the events of Australia in the year 1975 (an incredible year "down under," for those non-Australians among you) and was invited to talk about it on a breakfast television show. Did they want me to talk about what a significant and tumultuous year it was in Australia (which was the whole point of the book)? No, the producer was more excited by something else: *prices*. Everything was so much *cheaper* back in 1975. How could you not love a time when gas was only 56 cents a gallon? I went on TV and talked about the cost of living, as agreed. The hosts of the show were fascinated, reminiscing about that year with a sense of longing. I didn't have time to mention it then, but while people were paying less, they were also earning less. In fact, based on average income, most things were more expensive in 1975. When we look back longingly at the past, we don't always put it into perspective.

The most overrated decade of the past fifty years is easily the sixties (see #9), but looking at the past through rose-colored glasses has been a popular pastime since well before the good old days (whenever you think they were). The nostalgia industry is worth billions worldwide, which is a worry, because the word "nostalgia" is meant to describe a disease (which probably explains my queasiness whenever I hear 1980s dance music on the radio). A Swiss medical student coined the term way back in 1688 to describe "the pain a sick person feels because he wishes to return to his native land, and fears never to see it again." Simply put, it's extreme homesickness. "Nostalgia" now usually describes a wish to return to a time long gone, which we will *definitely* never see again. So a billion-dollar industry exists to feed . . . a medical condition.

As I write this, those rose-colored glasses are focused on the 1980s, with the television, movies, fashion, and music of the time making a comeback. The Ronald Reagan years in America are recalled as some kind of golden age (rather than a dark time of Cold War insecurity). *Xanadu*, one of the most notorious movie flops of the decade, was recently turned into a hit Broadway show. (The show's co-producer, Robert Ahrens, said that they were "trying to stay true to the spirit of the film—but nothing is perfect, so we're trying to improve on it." Thank God for that.)

Many of those nostalgic for the eighties are looking back fondly on a time when they were younger, prettier, and perhaps mortgage-free, but there are other consumers of eighties nostalgia who are too young to remember the decade. For them, it's a magical place like Wonderland or Oz that they can only dream of visiting.

Twenty years is the usual time that is allowed to pass before nostalgia properly kicks in. In the 1990s, we looked back fondly on the 1970s. Even derided symbols of seventies music (Abba and Donna Summer were reassessed as geniuses) and fashion (flared trousers came back, for heaven's sake!) were cool all over again. But did the seventies seem so special while it was actually happening? As a character once said in the *Doonesbury* comic strip in 1978, "Here we are, almost nine years into the decade, and the major cultural contribution of the seventies is a fifties revival craze!"

The fifties revival was a big part of seventies culture, returning to what many considered a far more innocent time (despite the Korean War, McCarthyism, racist policy, and everything else). In the seventies, TV shows like *Happy Days*, movies like *Grease*, and old-time rock 'n' roll groups like Sha Na Na made the 1950s, a very staid decade, seem far more exciting than it actually was.

(To show how confused everyone is, the extremely popular *Grease* was re-released with great excitement on its twentieth anniversary in 1998. Nostalgia for a 1970s salute to the 1950s. I'm not sure what this proves.)

If the 1950s were the good old days, what was everyone doing back then? They were watching musicals like *Singin' in the Rain* (at the movies) and *The Boy Friend* (on stage), set in the joyful 1920s; the most popular drama series on American television were almost all cowboy shows, bringing back the Wild West in all its glory; and one of Britain's favorite TV shows was a return to old-time music-hall theater (even the audience was dressed up in turn-of-the-century duds) called, naturally, *The Good Old Days*. Whenever you happened to be alive, things were always better in the past.

Indeed, one of the strongest times for nostalgia may have been the 1930s, when youngsters were forced to endure a craze for the 1890s—the last days of the much-vaunted Victorian era, the heyday of the music hall and La Belle Époque, well before World War I and the Great Depression, before the world was changed forever by horseless carriages and moving pictures. Nostalgia has always been with us, and it has almost never made any sense.

True, a few things were good about the past. There was usually less pollution, the Pussycat Dolls hadn't yet formed, and Dunkin' Donuts was still using fresh eggs in their dough. But the technological, progressive, and social innovations of the past few decades haven't been all bad. Maybe it's time we all lived in the present.

Why Things Aren't So Bad Now (Compared to the Past)

With rampant climate change, conflicts around the globe, millions going hungry, and the looming threat of terrorism, the world isn't perfect right now. But let's put it into perspective . . .

WARFARE

In the last century, wars killed 100 million people. No, that's not good. But if the same proportion had died in the wars of ancient tribal societies, there would have been 2 *billion* deaths. So despite all the world conflicts, we've actually improved, and we continue to improve. The Human Security Brief says that the number of battle deaths in wars between nations has gone from 65,000 a year in the 1950s to less than 2,000 a year in the 2000s. According to political scientist Barbara Harff, the number of campaigns of mass civilian-killing decreased by 90 percent between 1989 and 2005. Meanwhile, most conflicts are considered "nonviolent" by the Heidelberg Conflict Barometer. (Yes, it's called the "Conflict Barometer." Do you have an issue with that?)

WORLD HUNGER

There are still too many impoverished people in the world, but it's actually not as bad as it used to be. At the end of World War II, around 1 billion people were extremely poor. Now there are only . . . 1 billion extremely poor people. Okay, it doesn't sound like anything's changed. But don't forget: after World War II there were 2.5 billion people in the world, so 40 percent lived in poverty. Now there are 6.5 billion, so a mere 15 percent live in poverty. The World Health Organization says that 12.5 million children died in 1990, but only 9 million in 2007 (27 percent less). Right, we shouldn't get *too* cocky, but that's a start . . .

THE ECONOMY

As I write these words, everyone's worried about the global financial crisis. The 777-point stock-market decline of September 29, 2008, was a "record" crash, even worse than the infamous crash of 1929 (which, as we've all heard, led to the Great Depression). But if we talk percentages (which is the fairest way to do it), the Great Crash of 2008 was less than 7 percent, whereas the "Black Tuesday" crash of 1929 was 12.82 percent. What does this mean? Not much, really. On their own, Wall Street crashes don't lead to recessions (and certainly not to Great Depressions). Wall Street's worst-ever crash actually happened on October 19, 1987, when the Dow Jones industrial lost 22.6 percent of its value. While that wasn't exactly good news, it didn't lead to the Great Depression II.

DISEASE

In the past, we weren't faced with exotic new diseases like AIDS and Ebola, but we still had no shortage of diseases threatening to wipe out the world population. We had the bubonic plague, which killed half of Europe in the fourteenth century. We even had a worldwide influenza pandemic that killed 50 million people in 1918 and 1919. Health has generally improved, which helps to explain why our average life expectancy went from less than 40 years old a century ago to 66 in 2008. If you're reading this book, you have an excellent chance of living even longer (not because of any magical properties this book holds, but because that would mean you probably live in the West).

THE ENVIRONMENT

Okay, it's tough feeling good about this, as the world environment really is doing somewhat badly. Still, if you visit London (England), you might notice that—despite the much larger population—the air is considerably cleaner than it was back in the Victorian era, when the smog was notoriously thick and the city stank to high heavens. London's worst recorded smog, however, was much later, in 1952, when four thousand people died of heart and lung disease caused by the lead and sulfur in the air. Since then, the air has been relatively clear. Many other major cities, infamous for their pollution, have also been cleaning up their act. If we have the technology to pollute, we also have the technology to purify.

TELEVISION

If you think *How I Met Your Mother* is bad, put it in perspective by watching an episode of a "classic" sitcom from the past like *The Brady Bunch* or *Diff'rent Strokes*. (I'm just saying . . .)

OTHER BAD THINGS

Do you get angry (as I do) when you hear news stories about slavery, torture, human sacrifice, or cruel forms of entertainment?* A few hundred years ago, you probably wouldn't have cared, because all of this was normal and unexceptional. What about armies invading another nation, subduing the population, and imposing their rule and their culture

* By "cruel forms of entertainment," I mean things like gladiator contests and public punishments, not *How I Met Your Mother*.

on the hapless nation? For millennia, that's exactly how the world worked. If there were any protest marches or cries of international outrage, hardly anyone noticed.

‹‹

◆ ◆ ◆

See? Things aren't so bad nowadays. Of course, it's no reason to get complacent. We still need to save the environment, fix economic injustice, end world hunger, and produce a few more decent sitcoms. But it's not as hopeless as we might have thought.

1. Public Opinion

"It's what the people want!" Over the years, politicians have used that excuse for a good many lamebrained policies—and most of the time, despite being politicians, they were actually being *honest*. "Over 50 billion burgers served!" boasted McDonald's in 1985, suggesting that simply because something is popular it must be good. To paraphrase another common advertising line: "One zillion people can't be wrong!"

Well actually, they can. Apart from diseases, natural disasters, and very annoying animals like mosquitoes and seagulls, almost everything that drives you crazy in the world can probably be blamed on one thing: popular opinion. Don't like people ruining their health with Coca-Cola, supersized burgers, and caramel chocolate bars? They are only so common because so many people actually *like* them. Tired of Paris Hilton, Tiger Woods, and reality TV stars? If they weren't so popular, we'd never hear about them. Angry at the government? Unless you live somewhere like Myanmar (*aka* Burma) or North Korea, the government you are railing at is probably the one that received the most votes. As U.S. journalist H. L. Mencken said: "No one ever went broke underestimating the taste of the American public." Strangely, most of the world seems to share that taste.

At this point, you might think I'm being unfair to you, myself, and our fellow human beings. After all, most of the worst politicians in history—Emperor Nero, Attila the Hun, Hitler, Stalin—didn't come to power through popular vote.

Nonetheless, Hitler and Stalin were a hit with their subjects. "Uncle Joe" Stalin was loved by all—but then, his portrait was displayed everywhere, history books told of his unerring rightness, and every snippet of information happened to mention that he was a wise, omniscient leader. Faced with such information, it's likely that, given the opportunity, most people would have voted for him. It was not until after his death that his successor, Nikita Khrushchev, revealed that Stalin was, to put it kindly, an evil monster.

Hitler was also well liked. Between 1928 and 1932, the Nazi Party became Germany's most popular political organization, winning 18.3 percent of the popular vote in 1930. When he took over Germany in 1933, Hitler already had plenty of fans. The next year, upon the death of President von Hindenburg, an incredible 38 million Germans (that's 90 percent of them) voted Hitler head of state as well as chancellor, effectively giving him complete power (so while an election didn't bring him to power, an election ensured that he stayed in power). Ninety percent of the vote? Even Elvis was never that popular! Of course, the good people of Germany didn't know just how bad he would turn out to be.

That's the problem with people in general: *we usually don't know enough!* We might make decisions for all the best reasons, but we are not always well informed. Hitler and Stalin had many supporters who didn't know better. Ever since then (and well before), politicians have done their best to keep people uninformed or misled.

In fact, throughout the world there's a long, proud tradition of ignorance. To wit:

◆ In the ancient world, it was thought that the sun and the stars revolved around the Earth, that the Earth was the center of the universe—and believe it or not, the ancients thought that the world was shaped like . . . *a ball*! Yes, the ancients really thought that the world was round. Nowadays we all know that the Earth is an oblate spheroid (slightly flattened at the poles and bulging at the equator). How could anyone ever have thought otherwise? Gee, weren't our ancestors *silly*!

◆ How well have voters chosen their leaders? Well, let's take U.S. presidents as an example. A group of five hundred American history professors, ranking the presidents in 1991, decided (like many others) that Abraham Lincoln was the greatest. The *worst*, in order, were Warren Harding, Ulysses Grant, and Richard Nixon. For the record, Lincoln scraped into the presidency with 39.8 percent of the vote—the lowest winning percentage in history. So Americans were somewhat *lucky* to elect their greatest president. (Before you say, "Ah, but he had two rivals, not just one," note that *every* modern president has been elected with more than two rivals at the ballot box.) When it comes to electing *bad* presidents, however, voters seem to have no trouble. Grant had two landslide election wins; Harding's election in 1920 was the greatest landslide in American politics to that time; Nixon won 60.7 percent of the vote in 1972—at the time, the highest margin ever for a Republican president. At the time, despite a few conspiracy theories in the ether, the public didn't know about Watergate.

♦ What if you want to convince people of something unbelievable (as politicians are so often trying to do)? Well, fear can make us believe almost anything. When Orson Welles adapted H. G. Wells's novel *The War of the Worlds* as a radio play (in the style of a newscast), the night before Halloween 1938, hundreds of thousands of people across America ran hysterically through the streets, afraid that Martians were invading. Never mind that it was part of a regular CBS Sunday night drama series called *Mercury Theatre on the Air*. If it was on radio, it had to be true! Nowadays, of course, we wouldn't fall for it. We are now more familiar and skeptical (in a good way) of the media. Besides, the novel is too famous.

♦ Edward L. Bernays, you may recall, was the man who made women smoke cigarettes by promoting them as an effective weight-loss device and a symbol of equality. Proving that his magic didn't just work on the tobacco industry, Bernays also devised a campaign for the Beechworth Packing Company, a giant bacon producer, surveying five thousand doctors and dieticians, who promoted the virtues of a hearty breakfast. Alongside the expert opinion, his campaign announced that "hearty" meant bacon and eggs, rather than poisonous things like fruit juice and cereal. Since this campaign was launched, Americans have clogged their arteries at breakfast like never before. Faced with such brilliant PR campaigns, people around the world have damaged their health, their nation, and their planet in countless other ways over the centuries.

♦ In 1999, a British poll revealed that 61 percent of British teenagers believed in aliens and UFOs. A year later, a survey by *Popular Science* magazine found that 45 percent of Americans believed that intelligent aliens had visited Earth. Depending on your point of view, you must think either "What a bunch of crackpots!" or "What's wrong with the other 55 percent?"

In case you think that just proves that people were unenlightened in the past and we're much wiser now, please note the following fun facts from this very century:

♦ Before the diminutive South Pacific nation of East Timor won independence in 2000, the death toll from fifteen years of Indonesian occupation was more than one-third of the population—the highest per-capita death toll of any twentieth-century conflict. Grabs the attention, you may think, but the Australian media might disagree with you. East Timor is one of Australia's closest neighbors, but few Australians knew what was going on. Working in East Timor, journalist John Martinkus noticed that Australian newspapers didn't think the story was "sexy" enough. "Look, we are not going to publish anything on East Timor," he recalled the foreign editor of one major newspaper telling him. "Can you stop bothering us?" It helped that the Indonesian government of the time had employed some major public relations firms. However nasty you are, you can always find a PR firm shameless enough to help you.

- Nearly 26 million people voted in the 2001 British general election. That sounds like a good number of Britons exercising their democratic right, until you notice that, the same year, more than 32 million votes were cast—many, admittedly, by the same people—in the first season of the talent show *Pop Idol*. In the U.S. elections three years later, even with record voter turnout, neither candidate could draw as many votes as the finale (just the *finale*) of *American Idol*.

- In October 2003, seven months into the Iraq War, a study by the Program on International Policy Attitudes found that 60 percent of Americans believed at least one of several myths about the war. They thought that evidence had been found of links between Iraq and Al Qaeda; that weapons of mass destruction had been found in Iraq; and that world public opinion favored the United States going to war with Iraq. All of this had been disproven. When they want to, the mass media can mislead and misinform as brilliantly as any PR genius.

We can choose the person to lead us, the companies we support, and the food we eat. Occasionally, we get it right. Other times, we don't. There is simply too much information and misinformation out there, which could leave us a little confused.

Misinformation is a lucrative industry. There are around 140,000 public relations professionals in the United States—considerably more than actual journalists. But surely, these PR people don't all specialize in lies, do they? Well, it depends on whether you can believe them. According to a survey by the Aussie magazine *PR Week*, more than half of Australia's PR people have turned down a job for ethical reasons, a quarter of them confessed that they had lied as part of their job, 39 percent said they had "exaggerated," and 62 percent said that their clients had lied to them, so they didn't know that they were spreading lies.

Then there are the advertising and lobbying industries, which are also rather healthy. They do their best to make the facts simpler, even if they stop being factual. Thanks to advertising, millions of people have accepted that instant coffee is delicious, milk is an "essential" part of a healthy diet, taking the kids to McDonald's is a good way to take "a break," and Michael Jordan would actually choose to wear Nikes even if he wasn't paid millions to do so.

We will continue to fall for advertisers' claims, partly because we are presented with so much information that we'd like everything to be relayed to us in simple, easy-to-follow snippets. Even back in 1989, a few years before everyone was surfing the web, David Suzuki was already talking about information overload. "The problem is that we are inundated with information . . . but we have no idea how to wade through the morass and separate the meaningful from the trivial," he wrote, reserving most of his complaints for television. "We tune in and out, watching when something interesting comes up and drifting off at other times. By the time we go to bed, the contents of a four-hour viewing block may be completely mixed up, and it is easy to assume that a snippet remembered from one show was actually seen on another."

Since the web, misinformation has been even more widespread. Many people rave about how much the Internet has "democratized" the information world, and they may be right. Now if we want to spread news and information to millions of people, we don't even have to know anything! More people prefer to get their information from the bloggers (mostly commentators without the expertise), "citizen journalists" (reporters without the training), and those mysterious people who write Wikipedia entries. In his book *The Cult of the Amateur*, Silicon Valley entrepreneur and writer Andrew Keen recalled the day in 2004 when a web tycoon told him with excitement about the way that "noble amateurs" would democratize "the dictatorship of expertise." Keen suggested that he might have responded: "So instead of experts, we'll have a dictatorship of idiots." As a glance of the top 500 blogs might show, he would have had a point.

So here we are: ignorant, confused consumers (apart from the intelligent and well-grounded people who bought this book, of course). With all the information at our fingertips, no wonder we keep getting everything wrong.

BIBLIOGRAPHY

This brief catalog isn't an exhaustive list of books that I used when writing this one, but they certainly came in handy—or at least, will be useful to those who, for some reason, want to write a book exactly like this one. They will also come in handy if you want to read beyond the few pithy words I've been able to write about each topic. (They are definitely safer than using Wikipedia.)

Arikha, Noga. *Passions and Tempers: A History of the Humors.* New York: Ecco/HarperCollins, 2007.

Ayres, Ian. *Super Crunchers: Why Thinking-by-Numbers Is the New Way to Be Smart.* New York: Bantam, 2007.

Best, Joel. *Damned Lies and Statistics: Untangling Numbers from the Media, Politicians, and Activists*. Berkeley and Los Angeles: University of California Press, 2001.

Burnam, Tom. *The Dictionary of Misinformation*. New York: Harper & Row, 1975.

Emery, David, and Stan Greenberg (compilers). *World Sporting Records*. London: Bodley Head, 1986.

Gately, Iain. *La Diva Nicotina: The Story of How Tobacco Seduced the World*. London: Simon & Schuster, 2001.

Keen, Andrew. *The Cult of the Amateur: How Blogs, MySpace, YouTube, and the Rest of Today's User-Generated Media Are Destroying Our Economy, Our Culture, and Our Values*. New York: Random House, 2007.

Kruszelnicki, Karl. *Disinformation and Other Wikkid Myths*. Sydney: HarperCollins, 2005.

—. *Great Mythconceptions*. Sydney: HarperCollins, 2004.

—. *It Ain't Necessarily So . . . Bro*. Sydney: HarperCollins, 2006.

—. *Latest Great Moments in Science*. Sydney: ABC Enterprises, 1991.

Lloyd, John, and John Mitchinson. *The Book of General Ignorance*. London: Faber and Faber, 2006.

Shaw, Karl. *Royal Babylon: The Alarming History of European Royalty*. New York: Broadway, 2001.

Shenkman, Richard. *Legends, Lies & Cherished Myths of American History*. New York: Harper & Row, 1988.

—. *Legends, Lies & Cherished Myths of World History*. New York: Collins, 1993.

Stauber, John, and Sheldon Rampton. *Toxic Sludge Is Good for You!: Lies, Damn Lies and the Public Relations Industry*. Monroe (Maine): Common Courage Press, 1995.

Suzuki, David. *Inventing the Future*. Toronto: Stoddart Publishing, 1989.

Twitchell, James B. *Twenty Ads That Shook the World: The Century's Most Groundbreaking Advertising and How It Changed Us All*. New York: Crown Publishers, 2000.

Williams, Jessica. *50 Facts That Should Change the World*. Cambridge: Icon Books, 2004.

Wood, Michael. *In Search of the Trojan War*. London: BBC Books, 1985.

ACKNOWLEDGMENTS

Before now, I have never before included a special page just for acknowledgments in a book. This might seem very graceless of me, but I've always been afraid of missing a few people. Instead, I rely on the contents of the book (and the footnotes, if they say anything useful) to give readers an idea of who helped with the making of it. Also, I kept thinking about Academy Awards night, on which various people go on stage to accept their awards, boring most of the audience witless by thanking a long list of people. I didn't want to be so dull, especially as I haven't won anything.

But this time, due to all the people who have helped to bring this book to press, I'll break with a personal practice and adopt the respected tradition of giving due thanks to those who have helped. Or some of them, at least.

Firstly, I'd like to thank one of my fellow authors and journalists in Australia, Chris Sheedy, who tipped me that someone might like the idea for this book. I'd like to thank Meredith Curnow of Random House Australia, who first showed interest in the original version—and her colleague Katie Stackhouse, who took over the reins soon afterward. Katie also gave me plenty of ideas and discussed at length what should and shouldn't be included in this book.

Obviously, when mentioning a book like this, you are bound to receive many people's thoughts. I would like to thank all those people who provided suggestions and advice—some of which I used, the rest of which I was still grateful to ponder. As I said, I'm sure I'll leave someone out, but I should mention a few (in alphabetical order—an overrated but usually safe sequence): Chip Adams, Matthew Boulton, Peter Elliott, Joe Kenny, Aryavan Lanham, Eric Petersen, Susan Adams Robinson, Tony Starkey, Prachar Stegemann, Pushpendra Uppal, Veeraja Uppal, Christopher Willis, Salil Wilson, Alf Zollo, and especially [*insert your name here if I've forgotten you*].

I'd also like to thank Sir Paul McCartney—not because he had much to do with this book (though he is mentioned a few times), but because I'd like to make everyone think I know him. (To be honest, we've never met. Please don't tell anyone.)

Finally, I'd like to thank the late Sri Chinmoy, poet and author extraordinaire, who still gives me constant inspiration in my own modest writing feats.

ABOUT THE AUTHOR

Mark Juddery is a writer and journalist based in Australia, whose regular gigs include a blog for *Mental Floss* and a popular weekly column in the *Canberra Times*. He has also written plays, screenplays, and three published books. Like any sensible person, his great loves include music, film, history, and trivia.

Mark has run three ultra-marathons, has directed and appeared in his own short comedy plays around the world, can give a detailed synopsis of any *Doctor Who* television story, actually owns copies of most Velvet Underground albums, and occasionally tries to learn the mandolin (though it's best that you don't ask about that).

If you'd like to comment on this book, or suggest anything he's missed, you can follow his blog at http://50-most-overrated.blogspot.com.